I0112026

Breaking the
Healing Code

The Complete Biblical Journey to Discovering Physical, Emotional, and Spiritual Wholeness

Christopher-Charles Chaney

Special quantity discounts with bulk purchases for sales promotions, fundraisers, and educational needs. For more information, visit the author's website at www.AuthorChristopher.com, call (423) 781-1555 or write: CCM, 3712 Ringgold Road, Chattanooga, TN 37412.

Copyright © 2016 by Christopher-Charles Chaney
All rights reserved. This book or any portion thereof may not be reproduced or used in any manner whatsoever without the express written permission of the publisher except for the use of brief quotations in a book review. This book or any portion thereof may not be reproduced mechanically, electronically, or by any other means, including photocopying, without written permission of the publisher. It is illegal to copy this book, post it to a website or distribute it by any other means without permission from the publisher except for the use of brief quotations in a book review.

Limits of Liability and Disclaimer of Warranty
The author and publisher shall not be liable for your misuse of this material. This book is strictly for informational and educational purposes. The purpose of this book is to educate. The author and/or publisher do not guarantee that anyone following these techniques, suggestions, tips, ideas, or strategies will become successful. This book is not intended as a substitute for the medical advice of physicians. The reader should regularly consult a physician in matters relating to his/her health and particularly with respect to any symptoms that may require diagnosis or medical attention.

The author and/or publisher shall have neither liability nor responsibility to anyone with respect to any loss or damage caused, or alleged to be caused, directly or indirectly by the information contained in this book.

Although the author and publisher have made every effort to ensure that the information in this book was correct at press time, the author and publisher do not assume and hereby disclaim any liability to any party for any loss, damage, or disruption caused by errors or omissions, whether such errors or omissions result from negligence, accident, or any other cause. Views expressed in this publication do not necessarily reflect the views of the publisher.

Printed in the United States of America ISBN 978-1-941749-28-9
FourThreePublishing
Chattanooga, TN 37411

Copy & Development Editor: M.S. Moore
Editor: Mary Hoekstra

Unless otherwise noted, all Scriptural references in *Breaking the Healing Code* are from the King James Version of the Bible.

While the author has made every effort to provide accurate telephone numbers and Internet addresses at the time of the publication, neither the author nor the publisher assumes any responsibility for errors or for changes that occur after publication.

Dedication

ALMIGHTY GOD is truly the head, the salvation, and the rock of my life. He never ceases to amaze me with unexpected and undeserved blessings. When I look back over my life, I am stirred by the sheer thought of how God strategically placed a handful of key individuals in my life as I was growing up. By the same token, I am saddened by an oppressive consciousness of the little gratitude I showed to many of them when I was young. Some have said farewell to life without my sharing any appreciation for the colossal impact they had on my life.

In addition to surrendering praises to my God, I have learned to bestow flowers to those I appreciate while they are still breathing. With that thought in mind, I am truly grateful for two extraordinary ladies who have been solid pillars in my life: Odessa "Mama Peaches" Chaney, my biological mother, and Charlotte Hunter, my spiritual mother. The Lord used both of these incredible *ole-school mamas* to instill strength, determination, and tenacity in the very core of my being.

They also taught me to see each obstacle as a launching pad to seize uncharted opportunities. I have learned how to be thankful while eating beans and cornbread for a week;

how to stretch a dollar without bowing down to debt; and how to walk proudly wearing used clothes that did not fit.

These women taught me how to survive and how to dream. They are, indeed, my silent heroes whose mutual voices of wisdom, echoing God's, speak to my spirit every day. I proudly salute you both.

I am also thankful for all my younger brothers, James E. Chaney, Jessie E. Chaney, and Darrell W. Chaney; and step-brothers Wayne Cates, Corinthian Lee Cates, Antwa Lee Cates, and Kante Cates for inspiring me to achieve more than I could have ever imagined. I pray that each of my brothers will seize the generational mantle assigned to our bloodline so that they are equipped to walk unceasingly with their respective Kingdom-given purposes here on the earth.

I am also eternally grateful for both W. Joyce Brown of Phoenix, Arizona, and Brian Johnson of Knoxville, Tennessee, who have demonstrated the tenacity of standing on God's word until healing has been made manifest; thus, inspiring me to explore my own belief, to petition God for revelation, and eventually, to write this book. It is to you two that I dedicate this book with the sincere hope that you both will find the deserved treasures of comfort, peace, joy, release, and ultimately, your specific combination for breaking the healing code once and for all.

Preface

Are you continuously and hopelessly petitioning God for divine physical, emotional, relational, or spiritual healing?

Are you like many Christian believers who are moved during worship services to stand in the prayer lines because of a lingering sickness, disease, or terminal illness? When the call for prayer is made, you move from your seat to the front of the sanctuary. You find your place at the altar. Hands, which have been anointed with oil, are laid upon you. You listen earnestly to the words of the prayer, all the while hoping the minister will utter something refreshing and profound to cause your spirit to quicken with everlasting hope.

You are moved by the prayer as comforting background music fills you with a heavenly hope. A warm tingling sensation travels through your body. Could this be it? Could this be the final moment of your infirmity making way for the birthing season of healing?

The minister stops praying, asks if you received your healing, and with lifted hands, you cry out, "Yes!" With each step you take back to your seat to rejoin the onward looking congregation, you begin *convincing* yourself that your tormenting infirmity is gone. Behold, you are now standing in the manifestation of your long-awaited healing. You are overcome with emotion and hope. You are now in your seat. The call for prayer ends, the anointed flow of prophetic music ceases, the worship service concludes, and the warm sensation that tingles your rigid soul slowly subsides with each passing second.

Everything stops, that is, everything but the natural signs in your body or mind, which quickly remind you that the challenge or sickness still lives. Your hope of complete deliverance dwindles as you make your way out of the church doors while navigating through a sea of people in order to reach the parking lot.

Why me? Where is my healing? What am I doing wrong? You fill the throne room of God with silent questions and visible tears. You are wondering if God's perfect Will for healing is really for you.

Understand this. God's perfect Will is to never heal you. His perfect Will is that you never get sick. But because of sin, God gave us an alternative route to unearthing healing. His alternative route is His covenant or promise of healing. His covenant of healing is not only enough to prevent, but it also is enough to completely eradicate every sickness and disease from your life.

God's sovereign Word, combined with unwavering Faith, fervent prayer, and obedience allows you to walk in the entitlement of healing. Yes, as a believer, you are entitled to access the gift of healing and to walk in complete physical, emotional, mental, and spiritual wholeness. According to Psalm 103:3, God forgives us of all our iniquities and heals us of all our diseases. Not just some, but all of our sicknesses and diseases should be washed away by the eternal blood Christ shed for us at Calvary.

Breaking the Healing Code is specifically designed to help you seize your covenant and your right to healing by audaciously exposing known and unknown open doors that not only impede God's promise of healing but also thwart your Faith in divine healing. So no matter how many doctors you have seen, how many healing lines you have joined, how many prayer warriors you have sought, or the personal efforts you have taken, the healing answers you desire are literally pages away.

Visit www.AuthorChristopher.com for more information.

Biblical Definitions for Healing

Hebrew (Old Testament) definition for "heal"

Rapha' raw-faw' or raphah {raw-faw'}; a primitive root; properly, to mend (by stitching), i.e. (figuratively) to cure:-- cure, (cause to) heal, repair, thoroughly, make whole.

Greek (New Testament) definition for "heal"

diasozo dee-as-odze'-o; to save thoroughly, i.e. (by implication or analogy) to cure, preserve, rescue, etc.:-- bring safe, escape (safe), heal, make perfectly whole, save.

Contents

The King Desires Healing for You

*I have seen his ways, and will heal him: I will lead him also, and restore comforts unto him and to his mourners...**Isaiah 57:18***

The Lord is your Divine Almighty, your Holy Everything, the Sum and Substance of your healing. He desires to bless you in a hundred forms, at a thousand moments, across the landscape of a million years. Despite how your body feels, what the doctor's report reveals, or the number of prayer lines you have graced, sickness has a season, a purpose, and an end. The simple pages of this book are designed to fill you with strength and hope to overcome what is indeed reachable—*your ultimate healing.*

Could sickness actually pave the way toward the Lord's purpose-driven agenda in your life as a Christian? Why could not the Lord use sickness to demonstrate His power in your life?

After all, you cannot know left unless there is right; or know up unless there is down; or know cold unless there is hot. You cannot go fast unless there is slow, or know sadness unless there is happiness. Therefore, you cannot know the Lord's scepter of healing unless there is a season of sickness.

Even at the very dawn of creation, God never intended to administer a gift called healing. God never intended for man, the divine image of Himself, to become burdened or plagued with the spirit of sickness. The root of all sicknesses is sin. God did not create either one. After He beheld everything created, including man, He said it was *very good* (Genesis 1:31).

Thanks to the shedding of Jesus' blood on Calvary, God is able to do all things, including restoring you to the divine image of Himself, which includes perfect health in all areas of your life. He can do all things concerning that which concerns you – including neatly wrapping a timely message of healing in a book called *Breaking the Healing Code* and presenting it especially to you. God declares, "Healing is yours!" And He can do it for you.

There is only one thing that is *not possible* for God, and that is for God to not be God. God cannot *'not be'* God. Just as the attribute *wet* cannot be separated from water, God cannot be separated from His Glory, Word, and Promises. God is forever existing, so is His Word and so is His promise of healing for you.

Healing can be as simple or as complex as your Faith. God is not requiring you to perform for your healing by kissing a stone, chanting a chant, swinging a pendulum, saying a rosary, fasting for 40 days, or bowing to the East. God simply needs you to first believe by Faith.

According to Mark 9:23, All things are possible for those who believe. However, to fully embrace the belief of your Faith, you have to first know His Sovereign Will for healing. Secondly, you have to believe it for yourself. Thirdly, you have to accept the very thing you believe. Fourthly, you have to stand firm on *receiving your belief of healing* no matter what your body whispers to you or how loudly the doctor's report shouts at you. Finally, you must stand on your divine healing because it is a covenant, a right, and an undeniable blessing for the children of God.

Do you realize God wants to bless you far beyond your human capacity to tell Him how much you want Him to heal you? God expressed this by establishing a covenant with us in Deuteronomy 28. You are most likely familiar with this chapter of the Bible, but we sometimes overlook the condition in which the covenant blessings were rightfully released. You give all of Heaven the authority to release the blessings when you adhere to the conditions of the covenant mentioned in the very first verse of Deuteronomy 28.

There are three things you are required to do in verse one. First, you have to listen to the Lord; second, you have to observe or reverence His command; and third, you have to follow _all_ of His commandments. After you have satisfied these three conditions, the floodgates of blessings will open on your behalf. If you do not remember anything else after reading this book, remember the conditions set forth in Deuteronomy 28; especially remembering, to follow all of His commandments. And _all_ does not mean _some_ or _most_. All is ALL!

You are probably saying, "Pastor Chaney, I am doing all of that and still there is no healing for me." And you are wondering, "Why am I still sick?" Following and heeding the message of this book will take you on a trouble-shooting mission to uncover and expose doors that may be blocking your healing. After you understand _why_ you may be sick, we will advance to the next level. I will share with you, in the words of this book, valuable Kingdom _Healing_ Keys. These keys will reveal _how_ your healing can begin to spring forth when they are applied.

Understanding the *why* and the *how* allows you to embrace the process of healing with patience as you gain the strength to move far beyond any rejection, shame, or isolation. The Kingdom Keys are important because they are vitally instrumental in combating rejection, shame, and isolation – which are often associated with Christians who fall victim to lingering illnesses, infirmities, and disabilities.

2

What is Hindering Your Healing?

*....he gave them power (against) unclean spirits, to cast them out, and to heal all manner of sickness and all manner of disease... **Matthew 10:1***

As you may be discovering, the Old and New Testaments and contemporary testimonies about healing, taken together, provide comprehensive evidence that God's Word heals. His Word healed yesterday, is healing today, and will heal forevermore. Now that you have learned this marvelous truth, ask yourself, "What is hindering my healing?"

In this chapter, you and I will gently and carefully pull back the bandages to expose the common spiritual infections that are attacking your wellness. Are you ready to discover what is holding you back from living a more vibrant and healthy life?

Great. Let us find the answers together.

Let us start with the crucifixion of Jesus Christ on Calvary. A strange thing happened during the crucifixion. It had never happened before the crucifixion, and has not happened since. The veil of the temple was mysteriously ripped, top to bottom. The veil was what separated the main part of the temple from the Holy of Holies where the Ark of the Covenant was placed.

Essentially and symbolically, God removes every barrier that prevents you from entering into the Holy of Holies so you can receive wholeness. It is not God who prevents us from entering the spiritual place of healing, it is our own sins that stitch the veil back together and seal the doors to everlasting hope.

Do not despair! There are some common *healing* hindrances that I am going to tell you about. Learning about these hindrances provides the insight you will need to destroy ruthless spirits that are strategically positioned to wreak havoc on your physical, spiritual, and mental health.

Before I share these hindrances with you, please understand that there are many sicknesses and diseases that have no known medical cure. These are psychosomatic attacks on the spirit and they have consequences that are both psychological and physical. A psychosomatic condition occurs when a person believes he or she has real physical symptoms of an illness that often are severe enough for the person to seek medical help. After a medical examination and investigation, though, no medically recognized illness can be linked to the physical symptoms.

Sometimes a person's symptoms may go away or appear to have gone away. Other times, the person may continue seeking medical help because he or she is 100% certain the symptoms are real and serious. But many times, the medical doctor has a challenge identifying the condition or the root cause of the sickness. Therefore, symptoms are frequently treated with drugs that have side effects. Now, the person undergoing treatment needs additional drugs to counteract or neutralize the side effects. This vicious cycle only perpetuates sickness rather than removing it.

Why is the sickness being perpetuated and sometimes complicated with compounded side effects? Why is the treatment unsuccessful? Sadly, the treatment is often ineffective because it addresses natural symptoms, which can be seen, but not the root causes, which are often not seen. While the medical doctors are combating the evidence seen in the flesh and blood (the natural), there are often spiritual implications that represent the core root cause to the sickness. We think treating the robe of flesh is the cure to health and life, but God says to put on the Robe of Righteousness and receive all of its benefits, including healing. So God wants you to put on spiritual righteousness and fight? Yes, fight for your healing.

> Sometimes you have to *super* your *natural* in order to gain ultimate victory…

Though you may have natural symptoms of sickness, sometimes you have to *super* your *natural* in order to gain ultimate victory, which results in your ultimate healing. You have to become supernatural by fighting spiritually. Fighting spiritually allows you to move beyond symptomatic natural causes or the enemy's decoys. When you unmask the spiritual root causes and deal with them accordingly, you maximize the chances of receiving healing because there are no open doors for the spirit of infirmity to enter, to dwell, and sometimes, to hide out. The spirit of infirmity has *no legal right* to come near your temple, but it will do what is necessary to serve as a hindrance to your healing.

As you learn about healing hindrances in this chapter, you will be able to do your own troubleshooting to identify spiritual influences that contribute to your hurting or ailing. Once you have made that discovery, you will be free to devise a plan for supernatural deliverance. Once and for all, you will close the doors of hindrances behind you, one by one. Even better than shutting those doors, you will have the great pleasure of covering them over, top to bottom, with bricks and mortar, forever sealing them tightly for yourself and for all the generations to come.

As you read through this section, take an introspective journey. Be completely and totally honest with yourself. Do not be too quick to declare that you are free of any particular listed traits that could possibly hinder you. Pray. Ask God to allow you to see your real, true self. Ask Him to reveal your personal strategy for passing through and eliminating each of these hindrances from you and your descendants.

Understanding where you are in the Spirit ought to be one of your best weapons for defeating and destroying sicknesses and diseases. I will help you find out where you are by sharing this list of common hindrances for you to review:

1. Ignorance and unbelief

2. An unforgiving heart

3. Sin (including demonic influences, curses, and sexual immorality)

4. Impatience

5. A religious spirit (including pride and neglecting natural health laws)

6. Failing to realize the mysteries of our Sovereign God

7. Dishonoring leaders

8. A broken spirit

9. Fear (including anxiety and stress)

10. Neglecting praying and fasting (including not discerning the Lord's body)

Now, let us look at each of these 10 common healing hindreances, one by one.

1. Ignorance and unbelief

Did you know that sometimes God's blessings are not received? Sometimes we do not receive God's blessings because we do not realize or fully grasp the breadth, length, depth, and height of our true inheritance. God's people are destroyed by lack of knowledge (Hosea 4:6). To have knowledge of God is to be intimate with God. God's people are assailed and destroyed on spiritual, emotional, mental, financial, and physical fronts because they do not have an intimate knowledge. God wants us to be intimate with him. Contrary to popular belief, however, knowledge is NOT power, as the saying goes. It is *applied knowledge or intimacy with God* that is true power. So now the next question I want to ask you is, "How do you gain Faith in the knowledge of spiritual things and how do you apply them?"

> Contrary to popular belief, however, knowledge is NOT power, as the saying goes. It is *applied knowledge or intimacy with God,* that is true power.

First and foremost, go to a place of worship where you can hear the untainted word of God (Romans 10:14). The pure Word of God represents an incorruptible seed

(Luke 8:11; 1 Peter 1:23) in your life. If you are not being challenged by the Word of God, you need to re-evaluate your personal efforts toward knowing God. You need to also re-evaluate your efforts toward knowing your place of worship. As the Word, the incorruptible seed, takes root in your life, it will steadily grow and propel you to move forward while you bear visibly *good* fruit. If you are not bearing good fruit, then you must ask yourself if you are truly hearing and applying the Word.

Faith comes by hearing, specifically and solely hearing the Word (Roman 10:17). Notice this Scripture repeats the word *hearing*. When God repeats anything, there is a significant meaning, and that should be your clue to ask for deeper revelation.

The first hearing is embracing the words of God that are lifted from the pages of the Holy Bible and are spoken into the atmosphere. The second hearing is allowing God to speak and convey deeper meaning into your spirit. This is the level of revelation that often provides direct insight for your specific situation.

Through the second hearing of the Word, God may give you the knowledge of your healing. He may instruct you with the wisdom you need to stop taking a particular medicine. Through the second hearing of the Word, God may direct you to the right doctor, expose you to a natural remedy, or enlighten you with greater knowledge. Your complete hearing combined with your Faith in His Word is your personal remedy to combat ignorance and unbelief.

Now, I want to share some Scriptural references, comments, and a victory prayer to help you close the door to traces of ignorance and unbelief in your life:

And when they were come to the multitude, there came to him a certain man, kneeling down to him, and saying, Lord, have mercy on my son: for he is lunatic, and sore vexed: for ofttimes he falleth into the fire, and oft into the water. And I brought him to thy disciples, and they could not cure him. Then Jesus answered and said, O faithless and perverse generation, how long shall I be with you? how long shall I suffer you? bring him hither to me.

And Jesus rebuked the devil; and he departed out of him: and the child was cured from that very hour. Then came the disciples to Jesus apart, and said, Why could not we cast him out? And Jesus said unto them, Because of your unbelief: for verily I say unto you, if ye have faith as a grain of mustard-seed, ye shall say unto this mountain, Remove hence to yonder place;

and it shall remove; and nothing shall be impossible unto you.

Matthew 17:14-20

Sometimes we do not get healed because we do not believe God's promise of healing. (Mark 6:5-6; Mark 11:23). As I mentioned earlier, this is why it is important for you to feed on God's Word, for Faith comes by hearing and hearing by the word of God. (Romans 10:17)

Then said Jesus unto him, except ye see signs and wonders, ye will not believe. The nobleman saith unto him, Sir, come down before my child dies. Jesus saith unto him, Go thy way; thy son liveth. And the man believed the word that Jesus had spoken unto him, and he went his way.

John 4:48-50

Some people will not believe God unless they get some kind of natural or outward sign that they can see, feel, or touch. Sadly, some people think they cannot hear from God unless it's a pastor or some religious leader who convinces them that they hear from God for them. Nevertheless, in the absence of tangible evidence you must know, without a wavering doubt, that God is real. You must believe that you receive, so no matter how things appear outwardly, believe what the Word of God says (Romans 4:19-21).

Thus saith the LORD; Cursed be the man that trusteth in man, and maketh flesh his arm, and whose heart departeth from the LORD.

Jeremiah 17:5

Trusting only in doctors and medicines because of your unbelief becomes an idol, a thing. God is not against our doctors but He is against idol worshipping. To avoid idol worshipping, you must apply your prayers, Faith, and belief that God will touch the minds and hands of the doctors as you are being treated to receive your ultimate healing.

Here is your victory prayer and declaration of knowledge and belief to do His will and stand firmly on His promise for healing:

Father, I have heard your Word but have not hearkened to all of your commandments. Forgive me for not consulting the wisdom of your Word regarding decisions in my life. You said wisdom is better than gold and understanding is better than silver, so make me rich in wisdom and wealthy in understanding, Father. I am not only increasing in wisdom when I hear your Word, but I am also an active doer of your Word. I believe you. I believe your Word. I believe in the divine purpose you have set over my life.

Please help me to always seek godly counsel and to not look to the world, ungodly people, or even myself, for answers.

Father, thank You for giving me counsel and instructions even as I sleep. My mind is alert with wisdom to do all things through Jesus Christ, which strengthens me and shields me from unbelief and ignorance. In the Name of Jesus, AMEN!

2. An unforgiving heart

When you do not forgive others, your heart beomes bitter with emotional, financial, mental, spiritual, and physical torment. Bitterness and the unwillingness to forgive are both sins that not only separate you from God but also remove your entitlement to your heavenly inheritance of healing.

> Your tongue can be transformed into a weapon of mass destruction through mere words.

Forgiveness was so important that Jesus asked his Father to forgive those who persecuted Him. The Son of God, who at the time was suffering and dying on the cross, asked forgiveness for those who had put Him there (Luke 23:34). Jesus recognized that He could not complete His assignment of dying for us as long as His heart was blemished by bitterness, unforgiveness, and hate. An unforgiving heart will short-circuit your Faith and hinder your prayers for true healing (Matthew 6:14; Mark 11:25).

Here are some Scripture verses and comments to not only help you choke off the passageways but also close the doors to an unforgiving heart in your life:

Therefore I say to you, whatever things you ask when you pray, believe that you receive *them,* and you will have *them.* And whenever you stand praying, if you have anything against anyone, forgive him, that your Father in heaven may also forgive you your trespasses. But if you do not forgive, neither will your Father in heaven forgive your trespasses.

Mark 11:24-26

In anger, his master handed him over to the jailers to be tortured until he should pay back all he owed. This is how my heavenly Father will treat each of you unless you forgive your brother or sister from your heart.

Matthew 18: 34-35

In addition to forgiving our brothers and sisters in Christ, we must also forgive ourselves. An unforgiving heart not only opens the doors to torment, but it also represents a warring principality under Satan's authority and influence (Ephesians 6:12). A warring principality under Satan has at least six additional kindred spirits, including resentment, retaliation, anger, hatred, violence, and murder. And murder does not always mean to slay someone, as in taking life from their body.

Did you know that you can assassinate or 'murder' someone by the words you speak (Proverbs 18:21)? *Negative* words can kill a person's character or reputation. In fact, when you speak negative words to yourself, you are slowly committing suicide by slaughtering your own self-worth.

Your tongue can be transformed into a weapon of mass destruction, launching holocausts and wars through mere words. Because of an unforgiving heart, your words can devastate marriages, annihilate families, destroy friendships, eliminate careers, assassinate hopes, shatter dreams, murder reputations, and more. *Never* underestimate the power of your words.

Warring spirits that are rooted in an unforgiving heart are not always obvious, but you can eventually see their evil effects. Here is your victory prayer and declaration to heal an unforgiving heart:

Thank You, Father, for your greatest gift, Your Son Christ Jesus, who came that I might be forgiven. I now walk in the way of my Savior and forgive those who have done wrong to me. As painful as it may be, I release them with my words and in my heart. As I release them, You are filling me with Your love to overcome the hurts and disappointments in order to help me to completely walk in total forgiveness.

By the power of Your Holy Spirit, I decree that I am set free from any demonic spirits of unforgiveness, bitterness, hatred, resentment, murder, violence, and anger. As I have forgiven, I pray that You will forgive me where I have wronged You. Finally, my greatest joy is demonstrating how Your tender mercy and forgiveness set me free. In the name of my forgiving Lord, Jesus Christ, I pray, AMEN!

3. Sin, demonic influences, curses & sexual immortality

Sometimes God's children do not get healed because unconfessed sins or iniquities are in their lives. What about you? Are there un-confessed sins, demonic influences, curses, or sexual immoralities in your life? This is the area some Christians do not want to acknowledge, yet Satan gains great victory because we do not recognize or accept that we are facing these strongholds. God will not hear your prayers if iniquity is in your heart (Psalm 66:18). You can abandon this stronghold of iniquity by

> Satan gains great victory because we do not recognize or accept that we are facing strongholds.

acknowledging that you have done wrong, by seeking repentance, and by asking for forgiveness. If you are able to do this, the act of possessing a sinful heart will not prevent you from receiving the salvation of healing.

> He that covereth his sins shall not prosper: but whosoever confesseth and forsaketh them shall have mercy.
>
> *Prerbs 28:13*

Here are some additional verses from Scripture, as well as comments, to help you forsake and close the doors to all sin, demonic influences, curses, or sexual immortalities:

> Christ has redeemed us from the curse of the law, having become a curse for us.
>
> *Galatians 3:13*

> If I regard iniquity in my heart, the Lord will not hear me.
>
> *Psalm 66:18*

> Confess your faults one to another, and pray one for another, that ye may be healed. The effectual fervent prayer of a righteous man availeth much.
>
> *James 5:16*

Now a certain man was there who had an infirmity thirty-eight years. When Jesus saw him lying there, and knew that he already had been *in that condition* a long time, He said to him, "Do you want to be made well?" The sick man answered Him, "Sir, I have no man to put me into the pool when the water is stirred up; but while I am coming, another steps down before me. Jesus said to him, Rise, take up your bed and walk.

John 5:5-8

Afterward Jesus found him in the temple, and said to him, See, you have been made well. Sin no more, lest a worse thing come upon you."

John 5:14

Demonic influences exist because of sin, as the following passage states:

Then Jesus called His twelve disciples together and gave them power and authority over all devils, and to cure diseases.

Luke 9:1

By the power of His mighty Word, you can learn how to master that demon who is attempting to be the master over you. Demons not only cause sickness, but they also hinder healing in every area of your life. Sometimes it is not just a matter of praying for healing; you may need to confront six demonic spirits who have been assigned to destroy mankind:

> ➤ The Demonic Spirit of Blindness: *Matthew 12:22*
> ➤ The Demonic Spirit of Deafness & Dumbness: *Mark 9:25*
> ➤ The Demonic Spirit of Oppression: *Acts 10:38*
> ➤ The Demonic Spirit of Depression: *Isaiah 61:3*
> ➤ The Demonic Spirit of Epilepsy: *Matthew 17:14-15*
> ➤ The Demonic Spirit of Infirmity: *Luke 13:10-11*

In addition to demonic spirits, lingering generational curses provide a pathway for continued sin. By *not* hearkening unto the voice of the Lord and observing and following all His Commandments and His statutes, you open the doors to demonic spirits and continuous curses that plague each generation and continue for generations to come (Deuteronomy 28:15-68). Someone has to break the generational curses over your family. Why not you?

Thou shalt not bow down thyself to them, nor serve them: for I the LORD thy God am a jealous God, visiting the iniquity of the fathers upon the children unto the third and fourth generation of them that hate me.

Exodus 20:5

The iniquities of our fathers can affect up to the fourth generation. Sometimes we do not get healed because we need to break a generational curse (2 Samuel 12:13-14; 1 John 1:9). When there is a curse in our lives, there is a reason (Proverbs 26:2*)*.

Flagrant and sexual sins only result in your destruction. Some people are under God's divine judgment because of their continued and blatant disobedience. Repentance is the only thing that will turn self-destruction and disobedience around.

Jesus healed a man who had an infirmity for 38 years. Most likely, the man's sickness was connected to a flagrant sin. Jesus told the man he was made whole and advised him to sin no more. Jesus also told the man that a worse thing would happen to him if he continued to sin (John 5:5). When healing comes, it is important that you align yourself with the Word in order to maintain the *rights* to that healing. If you do not take steps to maintain your healing from God, the curse of which you were delivered will be magnified, just like Jesus told the man.

Afterward, Jesus findeth him in the temple, and said unto him, Behold, thou art made whole: sin no more, lest a worse thing come unto thee.

John 5:14

Flee fornication. Every sin that a man doeth is
without the body; but he that committeth fornication
sinneth against his own body.

1 Cor. 6:18

It is reported commonly that there is fornication
among you, and such fornication as is not so much as
named among the Gentiles, that one should have his
father's wife. And ye are puffed up, and have not
rather mourned, that he that hath done this deed
might be taken away from among you. For I verily, as
absent in body, but present in spirit, have judged
already, as though I were present, concerning him that
hath so done this deed, in the name of our Lord Jesus
Christ, when ye are gathered together, and my spirit,
with the power of our Lord Jesus Christ.

1 Corinthians 5:1-5

God wants you to know that when a person commits
fornication he/she is sinning against his/her own body.
Fornication is voluntary sexual intercourse between
persons who are not married to each other. Adultery is
voluntary sexual intercourse between a married person
and a partner other than the married person's lawful
spouse. God's Word refers to both acts literally; both acts
are also used figuratively to refer to idolatry.

When a woman commits adultery or sexual sin, she
puts herself under a curse and defiles herself, according

to Numbers 5:11-13. A man should not use this passage of Scripture to excuse his sexual sin. If a woman is cursed, a man is equally cursed. Sexual sins open the doors to more sicknesses, diseases, and cancers (Proverbs 5:1-11; Acts 15:29; Romans 1:26-28). The Centers for Disease Control and Prevention (CDC) estimates that nearly 20 million new sexually transmitted infections occur annually in the USA, which translates into nearly $16 billion in health care cost.

If you are struggling with the spirit of lust, cast it out! You can do all things through Christ who strengthens you (Philippians 4:13). Do not allow Satan to convince you that this sin of lust does not matter, or that you are covered by grace. Grace should never be an excuse for sin, nor should grace ever be a justification for God allowing sin into heaven.

You are more than a conqueror. Has not God said it? Yes. So do not listen to Satan like Eve did. Do not be defeated by the voices of Satan in your head. In a battle rooted in the spirit of lust, you cannot operate with the senses of your body. You must be mortified by the deeds of the flesh so that your *spirit* prevails (Romans 8:13). When you walk in the completeness of the spirit, you become unmoved by the lust of the flesh (Galatians 5:16).

Now, here is your victory prayer and declaration over sin, demonic influences, curses, or sexual immortality.

Father, I confess my sins. You said in Your Word that

if I confess my sins before You, that You are a Faithful and just God who not only forgives my sins, but cleanses me from all of my unrighteousness, including demonic influences, curses, and/or sexual immortalities. I receive Your forgiveness and stand steadfast in the liberty in which Jesus Christ provides.

Your unconditional love and forgiveness have given me the Faith, will, and power to master that which once mastered over me. Thank You for creating within me a clean heart and continually renewing a right mind and the godly spirit dwelling within me. I receive Your power and strength into my life, and my victory over sin. In the name of Jesus Christ, I pray, AMEN!

4. Impatience or a lack of perseverance

You are approaching the midnight hour of your sickness, but whatever you do, do not abort your mission of continuously casting your Faith and prayers to God. Sometimes, we do not get healed because we do not persevere in prayer. We give up too soon because God has not moved in the way we expect, nor according to our timing. His ways are not our ways – His timing is not our timing (Isaiah 55:8-9). God exists in eternity, not in our natural dimension of time. In fact, time is subject to God; time is His servant. God can command time to slow down, speed up, or cease. Time bows down to God. So if God heals you in the next few minutes, next week, or two years from now, He will be on time. You just have to remember to PUSH:

> Remember, when you are impatient, God is being deliberate.

Pray

Until

Something

Heals

Puuusssshhhhhhhhhhhh!

Not all healings are instantaneous. Your healing may come gradually, over a period of time, as you learn to stand in Faith on His divine Word. God knows that healing us immediately could sometimes hinder the development of our Faith. As you pray and wait, continue to see your doctor, take your medicine, and prepare for surgery, unless the Holy Spirit leads you to do otherwise. Until God directs your path elsewhere, follow the doctor's orders while trusting in God with your whole heart.

Here are some Scriptural references, comments, and a victory prayer to help you close the doors to impatience:

Then He spoke a parable unto them to this end, that men ought always to pray, and not to faint.

Luke 18:1

And he said unto them, Which of you shall have a friend, and shall go unto him at midnight, and say unto him, Friend, lend me three loaves; For a friend of mine in his journey is come to me, and I have nothing to set before him? And he from within shall answer and say, Trouble me not: the door is now shut, and my children are with me in bed; I cannot rise and give thee. I say unto you, Though he will not rise and give him, because he is his friend, yet because of his importunity he will rise and give him as many as he needeth.

Luke 11:5-8

Do not fall prey to the *impatient people* syndrome, that is, people who want everything done in a hurry or right now. God cannot be rushed to do anything. Impatient people are people looking for immediate action and satisfaction, so much so that God's patient ways are bothersome. Remember, when you are impatient, God is being deliberate. Many times there is no shortcut, no instant answer, and no immediate solution. There is just long suffering, which is a fruit of the spirit. The way to become a spiritually mature and healed believer is to spend quality time in the Word. As you wait on the Lord, remember to praise Him, despite the advancing of time. Praise helps us to wait on the Lord (Psalms 65:1).

This is your victory prayer and declaration over impatience and a lack of perseverance:

Father, forgive me for operating impatiently concerning Your Will over my life. I am now seeking Your perfect peace and Your patience. Help me to lay down all my tangled thoughts, restless emotions and impatient motives in order to wait on You. Teach me to wait patiently for You to bring Your answers to my prayers.

I have the patience to wait so that I am renewed and empowered to mount up with wings as eagles, run, walk, and not falter in my divine purpose. Your Word chases away my worries, doubts, fears, and impatience. I release my Faith and my confidence in You that as I have asked according to my Faith, I have received, according to Your grace, the gift of patience. In the name of my Lord, Jesus Christ, I pray, AMEN!

5. A religious spirit, pride, and neglect of the laws of natural health

What is a religious and prideful spirit? That is an excellent question, so let me explain it to you this way: A religious and prideful spirit is a demonic spirit that declares war against the fulfillment of God's covenant over your life and your intimate relationship with Him. The key purpose of a religious and prideful spirit is to distract us, to make us think we are good, to cause us to be critical of others, and to miss God entirely.

> When you avoid listening to the wisdom of your body, you jeopardize your health.

You can miss your healing if you are asking for the wrong reasons, or if you are asking with a prideful heart or judgmental attitude, or if you are overly critical. You have to earnestly prepare your heart for the expectation of healing (Proverbs 4:20-22; Romans 10:17; Joshua 1:8; John 15:7; and Mark 4:14-29).

Here are some Scriptural references, comments, and a victory prayer to help you close the doors to religious spirits, pride, or neglect of natural laws concerning your health:

Then the Pharisees and Sadducees came, and testing Him asked that He would show them a sign from heaven.

Matthew 16:1

The scribes and Pharisees were "lying in wait for Him, and seeking to catch Him in something He might say, that they might accuse Him.

Luke 11:54

Now Naaman, captain of the host of the king of Syria, was a great man with his master, and honourable, because by him the LORD had given deliverance unto Syria: he was also a mighty man in valour, but he was a leper.

2 Kings 5:1:10-11

And Elisha sent a messenger unto him, saying, Go and wash in Jordan seven times, and thy flesh shall come again to thee, and thou shalt be clean. But Naaman was wroth, and went away, and said, Behold, I thought, He will surely come out to me, and stand, and call on the name of the LORD his

God, and strike his hand over the place, and recover the leper.

2 Kings 5:10-11

When you do not take care of your body or adhere to physical warning signs that something is not right, you open the door to sickness. Your body is a living organism and will often tell you when something is amiss. When you avoid listening to the wisdom of your body, you jeopardize your health. Your body may not be able to withstand today what you did to it twenty years ago.

In fact, your body may be reacting to what you neglected twenty years ago. At any rate, listen to your whole body. Not getting enough rest, overeating, having an improper diet, and neglecting exercise can have fatal consequences (Mark 6:31; Proverbs 23:1-3).

Here is your victory prayer and declaration over religious spirits, pride, and neglect:

Father, I come boldly before Your throne of grace for deliverance from religious spirits, pride, and neglect. I bind every demon and demonic spirit of Satan that would attempt to stop, hinder, delay, or interrupt my life in any way. I cast down every work of darkness and the spirits of religion who are assigned to hinder me from receiving Your will over my entire life.

I break every hex, curse, or vow, every spell, incantation, ritual, and the stronghold of prideful neglect. I break any other legal rights that the spirit of religion may have over my life and that of my family. I am free, and whom the Son has set free, is free indeed. I choose to receive the anointing to break the power of the spirit of religion right now in the name of my Lord, Jesus Christ. AMEN!

6. Dishonoring leaders

It is a fact that leaders do not always honor God with their decisions, but should you, as a Christian believer, still respect their positions of authority? Does Jesus require you to be subject to Christian leaders and secular authorities in your home, at work, or at school? According to Scripture, the answer is a resounding "Yes!" Whether we approve of their choices or not, the designated authorities in our lives have been appointed by God. According to Romans 13:1, *Every soul should be subject unto the higher powers. For there is no power but of God: the powers that be are ordained of God.*

This is inclusive of all and includes local, national, and global leaders. We can honor our leaders' positions but still disagree with their decisions. Anything short of honor for those in authority is blatantly violating scriptural principles and wreaking severe harm on God's elect, but is still an open door to sin that fuels the onset or the continuance of sickness.

Here are some scriptural references, comments, and a victory prayer to help you close the door on any mindsets that cause you to dishonor those who have authority over you:

> I exhort therefore, that, first of all, supplications, prayers, intercessions, and giving of thanks, be made for all men; For kings, and for all that are in authority; that we may lead a quiet and peaceable life in all godliness and honesty. For this is good and acceptable in the sight of God our Savior.
>
> *1 Timothy 2:1-3*

> Obey them that have the rule over you, and submit yourselves: for they watch for your souls, as they that must give account, that they may do it with joy, and not with grief: for that is unprofitable for you.
>
> *Hebrews 13: 17*

> Honour thy father and mother; which is the first commandment with promise; That it may be well with thee, and thou mayest live long on the earth.
>
> *Ephesians 6:2-3*

> And Miriam and Aaron spake against Moses because of the Ethiopian woman whom he had married: for he had married an Ethiopian woman. And they said, Hath the LORD indeed spoken only by Moses? hath

he not spoken also by us? And the LORD heard it. (Now the man Moses was very meek, above all the men which were upon the face of the earth.) And the LORD spake suddenly unto Moses, and unto Aaron, and unto Miriam, Come out ye three unto the tabernacle of the congregation. And they three came out. And the LORD came down in the pillar of the cloud, and stood in the door of the tabernacle, and called Aaron and Miriam: and they both came forth.

Numbers 12: 6-10

And he said, Hear now my words: If there be a prophet among you, I the LORD will make myself known unto him in a vision, and will speak unto him in a dream. My servant Moses is not so, who is faithful in all mine house. With him will I speak mouth to mouth, even apparently, and not in dark speeches; and the similitude of the LORD shall he behold: wherefore then were ye not afraid to speak against my servant Moses? And the anger of the LORD was kindled against them; and he departed. And the cloud departed from off the tabernacle; and, behold, Miriam became leprous, white as snow: and Aaron looked upon Miriam, and, behold, she was leprous.

Numbers 12: 7-10

And he went out from thence, and came into his own country; and his disciples follow him. And when the sabbath day was come, he began to teach in the synagogue: and many hearing him were astonished, saying, From whence hath this man these things? and what wisdom is this which is given unto him, that even such mighty works are wrought by his hands? Is not this the carpenter, the son of Mary, the brother of James, and Joses, and of Juda, and Simon? and are not his sisters here with us? And they were offended at him. But Jesus, said unto them, A prophet is not without honour, but in his own country, and among his own kin, and in his own house. And he could there do no mighty work, save that he laid his hands upon a few sick folks, and healed them.

Mark 6:1-5

Yes, there are times when you, as a Christ believer, must question human authority (1 John 4:1). If the law of the land clearly contradicts the Word of God, you are to obey the Word of God, first and foremost. God does not want you to gossip about your leaders' choices. Instead, you are to pray that God will change their hearts (Proverbs 21:1). If you do not honor your God-appointed leaders, including your father and mother, you may possibly open a door to sickness, which robs you of a peaceful life in all godliness and honesty.

Here is your victory prayer and declaration for those in authority:

Father, I praise You that I have the privilege of lifting up those in authority over me, my city, my state, my country, and this world. Forgive me where I may have criticized and complained instead of exercising my responsibility of seeking Your guidance in prayer. Thank You for building a spiritual wall of protection around the marriage and family of every national, state, local, and Church leader.

I pray that every leader will study, understand, and follow the principles of Your Word. May they realize that all authority comes from above. Convict me to be a godly leader always over those who are under my leadership and authority. In Jesus' name, I pray. AMEN!

7. A broken spirit

A wounded spirit is an injury or damage to the unseen areas of our being, which include the spirit and soul (mind, emotion, and will). Eventually, the unseen areas under attack will manifest in a visible sickness. According to Proverbs 17:21, a broken spirit

> You are *not a human being* — you are only *being human* until the curtains of eternal life are lifted.

dries the bones. It is important to note that the marrow in your bones contains a vital part of your immune system. If your spirit is broken or wounded, then your compromised marrow may potentially open the doors for stroke, high blood pressure, seizures, and other physical attacks.

Now, brace yourself for what I am about to say. Ready? Here it is. You are *not a human being* – you are only *being human* until the curtains of eternal life are lifted. You are a spirit with a soul and you are dwelling in a body. *Your body is not you.* It is a shell that contains your spirit and soul. What you allow your body to do will affect the health of your spiritual sensitivity. When your body embraces fear, depression, hopelessness, anxiety, stress, grief, sadness, oppression, and hatred, your spirit is broken and wounded. Your spirit was never designed to co-exist with such harsh and callous attacks. So your healing from a broken spirit must be rooted in the act of relying on God's word to completely restore, maintain, and guard your heart.

Here are some Scripture verses, some references, comments, and a victory prayer to help you close the door to anything that causes you to have a broken spirit:

A merry heart does good, like medicine, But a broken spirit dries the bones.

Proverbs 17:22

The spirit of a man will sustain him in sickness, But who can bear a broken spirit? *Proverbs 18:14*

The Spirit of the Lord GOD *is* upon Me, because the LORD has anointed Me To preach good tidings to the poor; He has sent Me to heal the brokenhearted, To proclaim liberty to the captives, And the opening of the prison to *those who are* bound; To proclaim the acceptable year of the LORD, And the day of vengeance of our God; To comfort all who mourn, To console those who mourn in Zion, To give them beauty for ashes, The oil of joy for mourning, The garment of praise for the spirit of heaviness; That they may be called trees of righteousness, The planting of the LORD, that He may be glorified.

Isaiah 61:1-3

A broken spirit can cause some of the worst afflictions in your life, afflictions so severe that you will end up exactly where Satan wants you, which includes financial, emotional, mental, physical, and spiritual devastation. When you are petitioning God to close this door of affliction (a broken spirit), it is *very* important that you receive emotional healing before any degree of additional healing can transpire.

Now, here is your victory prayer and declaration over a broken spirit:

My Savior Lord, despite my challenges, I receive Your unspeakable joy and everlasting peace, which pass all understanding. Every care, every weight, and every attack I lay down, and I follow You. In you I have the strength and the understanding to resist the spirits of anxiety, anger, envy, depression, bitterness, hopelessness, loneliness, fear, and guilt. I thank You for mending my broken heart today. I no longer have an emotional weight. And right now, I accept Your unwavering peace, which transcends all understanding and guards my hearts and mind. In Jesus' name, I pray. AMEN!

8. Fear, anxiety, and stress

Are you led by fear or are you led by Faith? If you are not familiar with the promises of God concerning healing, then when the doctor gives you a bad report, especially a report of a terminal illness like cancer, fear can potentially cripple your soul and bury your hopes.

Fear is a spirit that does *not* come from God. God gives us the power, love, and sound mind to rebuke a death sentence with sheer Faith. (2 Timothy 1:7, Psalm 118:17; John 11:4).

Fear is fatal. Any negativity resulting from fear breaks the spirit and burdens the mind, body, and soul. As documented by the medical community, fear, along with anxiety and stress, whether separately or together, targets the cardiovascular system. High blood pressure, heart arrhythmias, and heart valve diseases are some common conditions fed by fear, anxiety, and stress.

I will share with you these scriptural references, comments, and a victory prayer to help you close the door to the damaging effects of fear, anxiety, and stress:

For the thing which I greatly feared is come upon me, and that which I was afraid of is come unto me.

Job 3:25

Now Peter and John went up together into the temple at the hour of prayer, being the ninth hour. And a certain man lame from his mother's womb was carried, whom they laid daily at the gate of the temple which is called Beautiful, to ask alms of them that entered into the temple; Who seeing Peter and John about to go into the temple asked an alms. And Peter, fastening his eyes upon him with John, said, Look on us. And he gave heed unto them, expecting to receive something of them. Then Peter said, Silver and gold have I none; but such as I have give I thee: In the name of Jesus Christ of Nazareth rise up and walk. And he took him by the right hand, and lifted him up: and immediately his feet and ankle bones received strength.

Acts 3:1-7

Here is your victory prayer over fear, anxiety, and stress:

Father, I boldly bind the spirit of fear and break every evil covenant that has brought fear into my life. Thank You for Your Spirit of boldness, love, and sound mind that enables me to conquer all things. All negative doors that were opened in the past by the spirit of fear, anxiety, stress, and other kindred spirits are at once permanently closed and sealed forevermore. I charge warring angels to stand guard to ensure that the doors to these unwanted spirits are never again open. In the name of Jesus Christ, I pray, AMEN!

9. **Neglecting praying and fasting** (including not discerning the Lord's body)

Praying and fasting

One of the most powerful spiritual weapons you have on earth is the combination of prayer and fasting. Prayer is never your preparation for spiritual warfare. Prayer *is* spiritual warfare in action!

In addition to or combination with praying, you enhance your spiritual power and alignment with God by fasting. What is fasting? It is the act of abstaining from food, drink, or other items (or activities) of joy for a period of time in order to pray and seek and hear the voice of God. Fasting takes a lot of discipline and strength. True fasting forces your *robe of flesh* into humility and breaks the power of ungodly forces. Fasting kills unbelief and brings answers to your prayers when nothing else is successful.

This is where the power is because the act of fasting puts us in harmony with an All Powerful God who demands humility from those who wish to be close to Him. Fasting humbles the flesh and the power of demonic forces. When you allow prayer and fasting to humble your flesh and align you with Heaven, it pleases the Spirit of God (Matthew 6). What better can you possibly hope to do than to please Almighty God?

The Bible is peppered with stories of many godly men who combined the powers of prayer and fasting. Moses prayed and fasted 80 days. Elijah prayed and fasted 40 days. Jesus, the Son of God, was a man of fasting and prayer (Matthew 4:2). So was the Apostle Paul (2 Corinthians 11:27).

So, let us talk more about the power of petitioning God through fasting. Often the answers we seek from God not only come, but come more quickly, when we fast. The Bible records men and women of great Faith who prayed and fasted until they received an answer from the Lord (Exodus 34:28; 1 Kings 19:8; Daniel 9:3; Daniel 10:2-3; 2 Corinthians 11:27; Matthew 4:2; Mark 2:18-20; James 4:8).

By fasting, we abstain primarily from food, and in some cases, water. A fast could be one day, multiple days or whatever God ordains for you. Fasting separates you from foods, items (such as electronic devices), and/or activities you truly enjoy. You sacrifice your enjoyment of pleasurable things to get in the face of God so you can hear clearly from Him. However, the Body of Christ must use the wisdom of God, which will tell them, in most cases, to consult with their doctors, particularly when making commitments to strict fasts that are prolonged and/or include the absence of water and medicines.

When we subject our bodies to a fast, we remove the distractions of the flesh in order to get in the presence of God. When we are in the presence of God, we have a better opportunity to hear His voice of wisdom. Fasting will give us God's focus for what we need, including our physical, emotional, relational, and spiritual healing.

I know you are probably asking, what are the fasting options for Christians? Are they mentioned in the Bible? I am glad you asked because this next section will answer your questions.

Here are fasting options for you to consider, along with your commitment to prayer:

➤ **Daniel Fast** – This type of fast requires no meat or animal products, no sweets, bread, dairy, caffeine, processed foods, or foods with additives. Only vegetables, fruits, beans, whole grains, legumes, and water are allowed. The Daniel Fast is usually set for 21 days (Daniel 10: 3-13).

➤ **Full Fast** – This type of fast only allows water. All foods and juices are totally eliminated. Pray to God for wisdom. Talk to your doctor, especially if the fast will be prolonged and void of any prescribed medicines.

➤ **One-day Fast** – This type of fast is only limited to one day a week and it only allows water or juice. This type of fast could also include eliminating something you enjoy, such as talking on the cell phone, surfing the internet, spending time on social media, or playing video games.

➤ **Partial Fast** - A partial fast is normally from 6:00 am to 3:00 pm, or from sunup to sundown. There are three variations of this fast: 1) Full fast; 2) vegetables and fruits only; or 3) the elimination of certain food types, such as sodas, coffee, or pastries.

➤ **Social Fast** – This fast requires the participant to avoid using the cell phone, Facebook, iPad, computer, television, or other types of social and social media enjoyments. Rather than *Faithfully* connecting to the world, you should spend concentrated time connecting with God by studying the Bible, praying, meditating, praising Him, or worshiping Him. Pray to God and ask for the appropriate duration of your social fast. It could be an hour for a week, it could be 4 hours on a given day, or it could be an entire weekend.

At least six types of fasting are referenced throughout the Bible. They include:

> ➢ **3 Day Fast**
>   Old Testament References:
>   *Esther 4:13-16, 5:1, 9:3*
>
>   New Testament References:
>   *Matthew 15:22-29; Acts 9:9, 17*

> ➢ **7 Day Fast**
>   Old Testament References:
>   *II Samuel 12:16-23; I Samuel 31:13*

> ➢ **14 Day Fast**
>   New Testament Reference:
>   *Acts 27:33, 34*

> ➢ **21 Day Fast**
>   Old Testament Reference:
>   *Daniel 10:3-13*

> ➢ **40 Day Fast**
>   Old Testament References:
>   *Deuteronomy 9:9, 18, 25-29, 10:10,*
>   *Exodus 24:13-18, 32:15-17; I Kings 19:7-18*
>
>   New Testament Reference:
>   *Matthew 4:1-11*

➤ **Corporate Fast**
Old Testament References:
*1 Samuel 7:5-6; Ezra 8:21-23; Nehemiah. 9:1-3,
Joel 2:15-16; Jonah 3:5-10*

New Testament Reference:
Acts 27:33-37

I am a minister of the gospel, author, and friend, but not a doctor. Here is my disclaimer for you. Before you choose to fast, exercise due diligence by praying and seeking sufficient counsel from the Bible. In some cases, you may want to also seek counsel from your medical doctor. Always use wisdom before you commit to fasting.

Let me share some additional Scriptures for you that address fasting and prayer:

Is not this the fast that I have chosen? to loose the bands of wickedness, to undo the heavy burdens, and to let the oppressed go free, and that ye break every yoke? Is it not to deal thy bread to the hungry, and that thou bring the poor that are cast out to thy house? when thou seest the naked, that thou cover him; and that thou hide not thyself from thine own flesh? Then shall thy light break forth as the morning, and thine health shall spring forth speedily: and thy righteousness shall go before thee; the glory of the LORD shall be thy reward.

Isaiah 58:6-8

And Jesus rebuked the devil; and he departed out of him: and the child was cured from that very hour. Then came the disciples to Jesus apart, and said, Why could not we cast him out? And Jesus said unto them, Because of your unbelief: for verily I say unto you, If ye have faith as a grain of mustard seed, ye shall say unto this mountain, Remove hence to yonder place; and it shall remove; and nothing shall be impossible unto you. Howbeit this kind goeth not out but by prayer and fasting.

Matthew 17:18-21

Often there is no healing because we have not aggressively sought God in prayer and fasting. Sometimes we are not praying in complete Faith when seeking God for our healing.

And the prayer of faith shall save the sick, and the Lord shall raise him up; and if he have committed sins, they shall be forgiven him.

James 5:15

Sometimes we do not get healed because we do not expect to receive anything from God or we simply do not ask.

Ye lust, and have not: ye kill, and desire to have, and cannot obtain: ye fight and war, yet ye have not, because ye ask not.

James 4:2

For this cause many are weak and sickly among you, and many sleep. For if we would judge ourselves, we should not be judged. But when we are judged, we are chastened of the Lord, that we should not be condemned with the world."

Corinthians 11:30

Discerning the Lord's Body

Many Christians have not discerned the physical and spiritual aspect of the Lord's Body.

First, some people do not receive and accept all churches that claim Jesus Christ as Savior. When we do not love our brothers and sisters in the Lord, we do not properly discern His Body. When we walk with intolerance or un-forgiveness against a church or a fellow church member in the Lord, we are not discerning His Body properly.

Second, some do not properly discern what His physical body represented. The back of Jesus, our Savior's body, took stripes with barbed strips of a whip for our healing (1 Peter 2:24). His brutally beaten body underwent a burial, and then came His glorious resurrection.

According to 1 Corinthians 11:30, the lack of discernment of what our Lord did for us with His Body leaves many people not only weak and sickly in the church, but some even sleep, as in being in a state of death. We must properly discern all aspects of the Lord's Body. Why? On the eve of His death, Jesus instituted a significant new fellowship meal, which has become an integral part of our Christian worship. It allows us to remember our Savior's courageous death and victorious resurrection. In fact, in Exodus 12, God commanded us to practice this Passover feast, Communion, throughout all nations.

Many Christians have not discerned the physical and spiritual aspect of the Lord's

The Passover commemorates the final plague in which all of the firstborn children died in the land of Egypt. The firstborn children of the Hebrew nation were spared because the Hebrews sprinkled the blood of a lamb on their doorposts. The lamb was then roasted and eaten with unleavened bread.

During the Last Supper or Passover celebration, Jesus took a loaf of bread and gave thanks to the Father. As He broke it and gave it to His disciples, He said, "This is my Body given for you; do this in remembrance of me." In the same way, after the supper, He took the cup, saying, "This cup is the New Covenant in my Blood, which is poured out for you." The Lord's Supper, our Communion, allows us to remember what Jesus did, as well as to celebrate His victory. The Lord's Supper is found in the Gospel Scriptures.

> And as they were eating, Jesus took bread, and blessed it, and brake it, and gave it to the disciples, and said, Take, eat; this is my body. And he took the cup, and gave thanks, and gave it to them, saying, Drink ye all of it; For this is my blood of the new testament, which is shed for many for the remission of sins. But I say unto you, I will not drink henceforth of this fruit of the vine, until that day when I drink it new with you in my Father's kingdom.
>
> *Matthew 26:26-29*

> The Son of man indeed goeth, as it is written of him: but woe to that man by whom the Son of man is betrayed! good were it for that man if he had never been born. And as they did eat, Jesus took bread, and blessed, and brake it, and gave to them, and said, Take, eat: this is my body. And he took the cup, and when he had given thanks, he gave it to them: and they all drank of it. And he said unto them, This is my blood of the new testament, which is shed for many. Verily I say unto you, I will drink no more of

the fruit of the vine, until that day that I drink it new in the kingdom of God.

Mark 14:21-25

And he said unto them, With desire I have desired to eat this passover with you before I suffer: For I say unto you, I will not any more eat thereof, until it be fulfilled in the kingdom of God. And he took the cup, and gave thanks, and said, Take this, and divide it among yourselves: For I say unto you, I will not drink of the fruit of the vine, until the kingdom of God shall come. And he took bread, and gave thanks, and brake it, and gave unto them, saying, This is my body which is given for you: this do in remembrance of me. Likewise also the cup after supper, saying, This cup is the new testament in my blood, which is shed for you. But, behold, the hand of him that betrayeth me is with me on the table. And truly the Son of man goeth, as it was determined: but woe unto that man by whom he is betrayed!

Luke 22:15-22

When you take Communion, you are identifying with Jesus Christ. **When you take the bread, you consume His body. When you take the wine, you consume His blood. You activate a blood covenant that has a specific**

covenant agreement: The Lord provides healing and you walk in obedience. That is the covenant agreement. The spirit of infirmity or plague of sickness and death will *pass over* you just as it did for the Children of Israel. According to Psalm 105:37, none of God's chosen Children were feeble, meaning none were sick or diseased, after participating in the first Passover. You can walk in the same blessed hope.

According to Exodus 12:37–38, the Israelites numbered nearly six hundred thousand men on foot, not including women and children, plus many non-Israelites and livestock were among them. Numbers 1:46 gives a more precise total of 603,550 men aged 20 and up. The 600,000 plus wives, children, the elderly and the *mixed multitude* of non-Israelites could have numbered as many as 2 million people, according to some Biblical scholars. Imagine, 2 million people all healed! Now, that is a revival! And that is His faithful blood covenant of healing in action!

I cannot emphasize this enough: when you consume Communion, you consume Christ. You and Christ are one. When you sin, you break the blood covenant of healing. Then, the spirit of sickness or plague of sickness and death have an open door to viciously attack you, just like it did the firstborn of Egypt. The Egyptian households, where there were firstborn children, had no blood covering. So they were vulnerable, or subject to the spirit of death, who had a specific assignment: to kill only the firstborn. The spirit of sickness and death had specific assignments to bring instant death or to torment until death was achieved.

The Blood of Jesus Christ has a specific assignment as well. It is to ensure that you are not feeble. The Blood of Jesus Christ can only do this to its utmost fullness when you are in right standing with the Lord. Today, the church does not fully reverence or understand the significance of the Lord's Supper, which causes a breach of God's healing covenant.

Here is your victory prayer and declaration when taking or preparing to take Communion:

My Lord and Master, if I have taken Communion without completely examining myself, forgive me. Whether I did it knowingly or unknowingly, I ask with a repentant heart that You forgive me. With a full understanding, I will now always fully repent before partaking of the bread, which represents Your Holy Body, and the wine, which represents Your Holy

Blood. Give me the strength to now properly partake of Communion so that there is no cause for sickness or death in my life. Now unto the King eternal, immortal, invisible, the only wise God, be honor and glory forever and ever. In the name of Jesus, I pray, AMEN!

10. Failing to realize the mysteries of Our Sovereign God

God's mysterious actions cannot always be explained; nevertheless, they can always be glorified. Oftentimes, there is just no answer to the question of why you or a loved one did not receive healing, or why you are suffering through hardship. Why the sickness, despair, and suffering? God's ways are not our ways, and neither are His thoughts our thoughts.

> Ask Job. He never knew what hit him. God never gave him an explanation.

God certainly and absolutely must know something we do not know. Ask Job. He never knew what hit him. The life of Job is described in the Book of Job, also known as the book of questions. Most of the questions were never answered. Job stood steadfastly in the face of stark tragedy, with unwavering Faith, as everything in his life withered away.

Before tragedy encircled his life, Job was prosperous on all fronts. He was not only described as being a perfect and upright man who reverenced the Lord, but he was the greatest of all men in the east. He was a devout man of God, loyal husband, and loving father of 10 children. As a wealthy man, he owned land as well as thousands of heads of livestock. His immense wealth also included robust health for him and those who were a part of his life.

Suddenly, without warning, Job starts to lose everything, including all his children, livestock, the health of everyone and everything, his impeccable reputation, and the support of his wife. Although Job suffered dearly and never got answers to explain what had befallen him and why, he never cursed God or wavered in Faith. God allowed Job to suffer in order to silence Satan. All the while, Job was never aware of what was happening in Heaven between God's belief in Job and Satan's accusations against Job.

Job had an open door that Satan used against him. That door was the *spirit of fear*, which, as I discuss extensively in Chapter 2, is a hindrance to healing. In Job 3:25, Job said, "For the thing which I greatly *feared* is come upon me, and that which I was afraid of is come unto me." His sons and daughters continuously sinned and cursed God in their hearts. Job was vexed with the tormenting fear of losing his children and persistently gave burnt offerings unto God for mercy (Job 1:4-5).

The mystery behind Job's tragedy was never revealed to him. Job simply knew God. Job simply trusted God, and in the end, God doubled everything that Job had lost (Job 42:10). In short, Job's suffering was for the divine purpose set by God, which resulted in Job receiving double for his troubles.

We agonize over suffering and plead for answers from a Sovereign God who works everything out for our good and for His Glory. Whether or not He reveals His mysteries to us on earth will not matter once we get to Heaven. Just ask Job.

Here are some Scriptural references and comments to shed light on the secret things of the Lord and sometimes, the suffering He allows:

Beloved, think it not strange concerning the fiery trial which is to try you, as though some strange thing happened unto you: But rejoice, inasmuch as ye are partakers of Christ's sufferings; that, when his glory shall be revealed, ye may be glad also with exceeding joy.

1 Peter 4: 12-13

Therefore I take pleasure in infirmities, in reproaches, in necessities, in persecutions, in distresses for Christ's sake: for when I am weak, then am I strong.

2 Corinthians 12:10

My brethren, count it all joy when you fall into various trials, knowing that the testing of your Faith produces patience.

James 1:2

To deliver such a one unto Satan for the destruction of the flesh, that the spirit may be saved in the day of the Lord Jesus.

1 Corinthians 5:5

The secret things belong to the Lord our God, but those things which are revealed belong to us and to our children forever.

Deuteronomy 29:29

And we know that all things work together for good to them that love God, to them who are called according to his purpose.

Romans 8:28

Then our response must be, as Job's was: "The Lord gave, and the Lord has taken away; Blessed be the name of the Lord.

Job 1:21

Here are your victory prayer and a declaration for trusting the Sovereignty of God to overcome the mystery of why we suffer:

Precious Father, help me to accept what I cannot change without compromising my patience and obedience to You. I welcome Your complete, perfect, and absolute Will over my life without interference, delay, or failure. Your ways are greater than mine, and I trust that everything is working for my ultimate good and Your ultimate glory. For Thine is the kingdom, and the power, and the glory, forever. In Jesus's name, AMEN!

3

Spiritual Root Causes of Sicknesses

*Behold, I give unto you power to tread on serpents and scorpions, and over all the power of the enemy: and nothing shall by any means hurt you...**Luke 10:19-20***

God does not send sickness to you because it is not His Will to do so. God desires that you have abundant life (John 10:10). So who is responsible for your sickness? Satan. Yes, Satan. But sometimes you are responsible. Sickness is often created by you, through the words you speak, the actions you take, the things you imagine, the thoughts you think, the emotions you feel, and the choices or decisions that you make. Other times, you may become sick or hurt because you are facing the spirit of infirmity, which is an *invisible* demonic weapon of mass destruction from the kingdom of darkness. The spirit of infirmity does nothing but fuel your sickness. To fully understand sickness with spiritual origins, you must dive deeper than your symptoms to uncover the root cause.

Let us look at an example. You are vomiting violently. You are developing a progressively higher fever. You are feeling fatigued and you have no appetite. What do you think you will say? You will say something negative about your current state of health. Right, you will be quick to say, "I don't feel good; I am sick." You immediately reach for the medicines that provide relief, even though you take them at the expense of their assorted side effects. The side effects occur, so now you need more medicine to combat the side effects. When the relieving effects of the first medication you took start fading, you decide to take another dose, and you now have the same side effects again.

You are caught in a vicious circle of seeking relief from sickness, but what you are experiencing may be the natural manifestations of a deeper cause that is invisible to the human eye—to your eye. If you do not know any better, you will pacify the natural manifestations of sickness with medicines, treatments, and even lifestyle changes, only to achieve the perception of relief. If it is a perception of relief or healing, it is an untruth from the father of lies (John 8:44) to divert you from the truth.

There are two types of sicknesses, and thus, two types of healing: 1) natural (or the physical world) sickness; and 2) spiritual (or the invisible world) sickness. Like most people, you often divert all your attention to the natural pain, hurt, or discomfort that you experience; you treat the natural manifestations of dis-ease with natural or physical means. Sometimes, you can successfully eradicate the pain, hurt, or discomfort and move forward with living life.

If you have tried everything imaginable in the physical world and still have not crossed the threshold of healing, then it is highly probable that you have been dealing only with the physical symptom of your discomfort. Now it is time for you to delve deeply into the spiritual realm to understand the *spiritual root causes* of your illness or infirmity. The continuous physical challenge in your body could be the result of you not yet facing those open doors or spiritual root causes for your condition.

Satan does not mind you getting a perceived natural healing or a physical, natural condition fixed. However, Satan really does not want you to be *spiritually* healed. Why? Well, Satan knows that once you are healed spiritually from the root cause into your spirit and onward to your body, you have a true deliverance of your spirit, soul, and body. Once you are spiritually healed and delivered, you close or seal the door of torment and you lock out Satan's access in that particular area of your life.

So, what exactly is a root? A root is a sustaining force lying beneath the surface. A root provides a source of nutrition for what lives on the surface. Like a tree's root system, you do not see it but the root system is vitally necessary for the very existence of the tree surface, branches, and leaves.

One of the biggest root causes of sickness or infirmity is fear, along with an unforgiving heart. Fear (including anxiety and stress) is the spiritual root of most of the chronic diseases and conditions listed on *The Spiritual Root Cause Matrix* at the end of this chapter. Fear is more than just a lingering emotion. According to 2 Timothy 1:7, it is an evil *spirit* who does not come from God. If you do not understand that fear is a spirit, you will arm yourself with the wrong weapons when engaging in spiritual warfare. In other words, don't arm yourself with aspirin when you need to war spiritually.

Here is what happens to your body when fear has set in. Fear is a basic survival mechanism that signals your body to respond to danger with a *fight or flight* response. As such, it is an essential survival instinct that keeps you safe. However, you can become incapacitated if you live in constant fear, whether from physical dangers in your environment or from.

perceived threats. Fear prepares you to react to danger by signaling your body to release hormones that slow or shut down many of your bodily functions

In some cases, fear causes your heart rate to increase, which provides more blood flow to your muscles so you are able to run faster. Your body also increases the flow of hormones to an area of the brain known as the amygdala, which helps you focus on the presenting danger and store it in your memory. Your brain is like a storehouse of memories, even with fear. You store it, recall it, and respond to it physically, mentally, emotionally, or spiritually.

When you are in a state of fear, your brain short-circuits your more rational processing paths and reacts immediately to signals from the amygdala. When your brain is in this overactive state, it perceives events as negative and even threatening, and that is how your brain remembers it. Your brain also stores all the details surrounding the danger—the sights, smells, sounds, time of day, and everything else. Those memories tend to be very durable, although they may also be fragmented, depending on factors like the fearful event itself and your level of functioning at the time, such as your age. Living under constant threat and constantly expecting fear weakens your immune system and can cause cardiovascular damage; gastrointestinal problems, such as gallstones, ulcers, inflammatory bowel disease, ulcers and irritable bowel syndrome; and decreased fertility.

Fear can impair formation of long-term memories and can cause damage to certain parts of the brain, such as the hippocampus, which is thought to be the center of emotion, memory, and the autonomic nervous system. Damage to the brain can make it difficult to regulate fear, leaving a person anxious most of the time. Additionally, fear can interrupt processes in our brains that allow us to regulate emotions, read non-verbal cues, reflect before acting, and act ethically. Fear can impact your thinking and decision-making in negative ways, leaving you susceptible to intense emotions and impulsive reactions. All of those effects can leave you unable to act or react appropriately.

The Word of God says that a broken spirit, which can result from being in fear, will dry the bones (Proverbs 17:22). The key word in this Scripture is *bones*. The marrow is located in the bones and is a link to the immune system. When the spirit is compromised *by fear*, it dries the bones or causes a physical reaction that compromises the spirit, and then subjects your body to fatigue, clinical depression, accelerated aging, and even premature death. So whether threats to your security are real or perceived, fear impacts your mental, physical, emotional, and spiritual wellness.

Chronic diseases and conditions such as heart disease, stroke, cancer, diabetes, obesity, and arthritis are among the most common, costly, and preventable of nearly all health challenges. In fact, heart disease and stroke are the leading causes of death in the United States. Both conditions are linked and rooted from high blood pressure. According to the Centers for Disease Control and Prevention (CDC), one in every three American adults suffers from high blood pressure, which costs the nation $47.5 billion each year. This total includes the cost of health care services, medications to treat high blood pressure, and missed days of work.

As you can see, heart disease and stroke have a root cause in the natural: high-pressure blood. And high blood pressure has a spiritual root cause, which can be fear, un-forgiveness, stress, or anger. As demonstrated by the following *Spiritual Root Cause Matrix*, many sicknesses and diseases thrive on the unseen fuel of spiritual root causes used by the kingdom of darkness in an attempt to kill God's people.

Spiritual Root Cause Matrix

Sickness/Disease	Body System	Suspect Spiritual Root(s)
Acne	Skin	Fear, Anxiety, Stress
Amenorrhea	Endocrine	Fear, Anxiety, Stress
Aneurysms	Cardiovascular System	Anger, Rage, Resentment
Asthma	Pulmonary System	Fear, Anxiety, Stress
Autoimmune Disease	Immune System	Bitterness, Rejection, Hatred
Constipation	Gastrointestinal System	Fear, Anxiety, Stress, Bitterness
Coronary Artery Disease	Cardiovascular System	Bitterness, Rejection, Hatred
Depression	Central Nervous System	Fear, Anxiety, Stress
Diabetes Mellitus	Endocrine	Fear, Anxiety, Stress
Diarrhea	Gastrointestinal System	Fear, Anxiety, Stress
Disease of Heart Muscle (Inflammation)	Cardiovascular System	Bitterness, Rejection, Hatred
Diuresis	Genitourinary System	Fear, Anxiety, Stress
Eczema	Skin	Fear, Anxiety, Stress
Fatigue and Lethargy	Central Nervous System	Fear, Anxiety, Stress
Frigidity	Genitourinary System	Fear, Anxiety, Stress
Hay Fever	Pulmonary System	Fear, Anxiety, Stress
Heart Arrhythmias	Cardiovascular System	Fear, Anxiety, Stress, Bitterness
Heart Attack	Cardiovascular System	Fear, Anxiety, Stress, Bitterness
Heart Valve Disease	Cardiovascular System	Fear, Anxiety, Stress
Hemorrhoids	Cardiovascular System	Anger, Rage, Resentment
High Blood Pressure	Cardiovascular System	Fear, Anxiety, Stress, Bitterness
Immunosuppressant Deficiency	Immune System	Bitterness, Rejection, Hatred
Insomnia	Central Nervous System	Fear, Anxiety, Stress
Irritable Bowel Syndrome (IBS)	Gastrointestinal System	Fear, Anxiety, Stress
Impotence	Genitourinary System	Fear, Anxiety, Stress
Overeating	Central Nervous System	Fear, Anxiety, Stress
Pain	Cardiovascular System	Fear, Anxiety, Stress
Rheumatoid Arthritis	Muscles	Fear, Anxiety, Stress
Strokes	Cardiovascular System	Bitterness, Rejection, Hatred
Tension Headaches	Muscles	Fear, Anxiety, Stress
Type A Behavior	Central Nervous System	Fear, Anxiety, Stress
Ulcerative Colitis	Gastrointestinal System	Fear, Anxiety, Stress
Ulcers	Gastrointestinal System	Fear, Anxiety, Stress, Bitterness
Varicose Veins	Cardiovascular System	Anger, Rage, Resentment

4

Ten Kingdom Keys for Your Healing

*To another Faith by the same Spirit; to another the gifts of healing by the same Spirit...**1 Corinthians 12:9***

Y ou have a healing covenant with Heaven. After all, God truly desires your healing and you truly desire to be healed. So where is the disconnection? Why is healing taking so long? While you are waiting on Jehovah Rapha, the God who heals us of all our infirmities, He has actually been waiting and waiting for *you* to move.

God simply will never *not* hear your petitions, for He confirms this in His Word by declaring that it shall come to pass. He will answer and hear long before you call and speak (Isaiah 65:24). God has heard you and He has the plan to deliver the gift of healing to your front door. In Matthew 16:19, Jesus said, "I will give you the keys of the kingdom of heaven; whatever you bind on earth will be bound in heaven, and whatever you loose on earth will be loosed in heaven." He has a plan for your healing. According to 1 Corinthians 5:17, you were made a new creature who has died to sin.

> As you pursue these Keys, you are pursuing God, who is the Restorer of the *healing* breach.

Are you completely dead to sin and alive in Him? When you become alive in Him, you are His beloved. He desires to heal so much for you, His Beloved, that He presents

Kingdom Keys to help you break the healing code. He wants you to walk in complete wholeness. Several Healing Keys of the Kingdom have been given because everyone is not on the same level of Faith. One person might be able to take the Word, speak it, and believe it without any outward evidence. Another person's Faith necessitates that someone anointed lays hands on or prays for them. Some people need something they can see, hear, or touch to receive healing.

No matter where your level of Faith is, always pray. Prayer is powerful. Pick up one, two, or all of these Keys and start unlocking the healing doors in your life. If one Key does not open the doors, pray and ask God if you should try another or combinations of others. Administering the right Key or Keys, combined with your Faith and obedience, could very well open the door or break the code, once and for all, to your healing. Keep asking. Keep seeking. Keep knocking. Keep using the Keys until the door of healing is open unto you (Matthew 7:7). As you pursue these Keys, you are pursuing God, who is the Restorer of the *healing* breach.

Here are the 10 Kingdom Keys God is offering in this season to help you gain or regain healing:

1. Using the Gift of Healing

2. Anointing with Oil

3. Using Prayer Cloths

4. Praying in Agreement

5. Exercising Faith

6. Laying on of Hands

7. Believing

8. Using the Name of Jesus

9. Meditating on the Word

10. Obeying the Instructions for the Lord's Supper

1. Gifts of Healing

God has put gifts of healing in the New Testament Church for you (1 Corinthians 12:1, 9). The gifts of healing could also refer to a variety of healings, from powerful demonstrations of sudden, miraculous, or dramatic healings, to the routine short- or long-term administration of medical treatments. The gift of healing could even be the ability to show genuine love or forgiveness towards another.

While there is some debate about the usage of the spiritual gift of healing in the Church today, God still heals. God can choose to release Divine Healing in your life by any means necessary. In fact, Salvation itself is a wonder-working miracle. Your eternal salvation is perhaps the greatest healing you could ever desire and receive. Salvation and healing are gifts that are available for you. In most cases, you just need to ask in Faith, stand on God's Word, and expect to receive the gift of healing.

2. Anointing with Oil

The sick can be anointed with oil. What does the Bible say about anointing with oil? In the Old Testament, the high priest, tabernacle, and furniture were anointed with holy oil. In Exodus 30:23-24, the major ingredients included myrrh, cinnamon, calamus, cassia, and olive oil and are recorded in Old Testament. Throughout the Bible, ancient priests, prophets, and physicians anointed people with oils and prayed with them for their spiritual purification, moral repentance, and especially their healing. Jesus and the Christians in the early Church did so too. In fact, here is what James 5:14 tell us about healing relative to anointing oils:

Is any sick among you? Let him call for the elders of the church; and let them pray over him, anointing him with oil in the name of the Lord: and the prayer of Faith shall save the sick, and the Lord shall raise him up; and if he have committed sins, they shall be forgiven him.

James 5:13:15

The Scriptures allow you to tap into three great healing sources: the power of praying in agreement; the power of walking in repentance; and the power of using special anointing or essential oils in the name of our Lord.

There is absolutely no power in the oil itself. Oil is just oil if it is not consecrated unto the Lord. The power occurs when we recognize the *anointed* oil as a symbol of His healing covenant to perform His perfect Will on the earth and within the measure of your Faith (Romans 12:3). It is God Himself, and He alone, who makes the oil holy in His glorious name. Be sure you pray over any anointed oil you have in your home and pray for oil that will be used as you are standing in the healing line waiting for prayer.

Here is an example of how to pray over the oil:

> Father God, I pray right now that You will anoint this oil in Your precious name. I pray that You will supernaturally cleanse it of any defilement that may be in, around, or upon it. I pray that You will make it Holy to demonstrate the work of Your Divine Glory in the mighty and matchless name of Jesus Christ, I pray, AMEN!

For more information about anointed oils of the Bible and essential oils, please email Kingshipanointing@gmail or visit www.AuthorChristopher.com.

3. **Prayer cloths**

Prayer cloths are handkerchiefs or prayer shawls that can be used as special healing anointings (Acts 19:11-12). In the Scriptures, prayer cloths or *handkerchiefs* were believed to have the power of Jesus flowing through them. It is not the *cloth* that is responsible for the healing. Without Faith and the works of God, prayer cloths are rendered powerless. The believer's Faith is in the power of prayer and ultimately in the healing power of God, which is symbolized by the cloth.

Now let us look at healing, Faith, and the cloth. When sick and diseased people simply touched a piece of Jesus' clothing, they were healed. In fact, Luke 8:40-48 shared the story of a woman who had been sick with an issue of blood for 12 years. She approached Jesus, thinking, "If I but touch the hem of His garment I shall be cured." And that is exactly what happened. The woman touched the hem of Jesus' robe and He felt His miraculous power flow through the garment, curing the woman. Jesus most likely was wearing a prayer shawl, and thus, the woman with an issue of blood touched it and was healed. It is believed that she touched the knotted tassels, or fringes, which are the most important part of the entire garment.

The prayer shawl or tallit is an important component of the Jewish Faith and history. It contains great meaning and symbolism, especially in the fringes or knotted tassels on its four kanaph. The kanaph are the corners or the wings of the garment. It is believed that the woman having the issue of blood reached out and touched kanaph, or one of the knotted tassels. The tassels represent the divine covenant of healing, which symbolizes the Messiah having healing in His wings. In Deuteronomy 22, God commanded the Jewish men to make fringes and wear them in a place that was visible to remind them of God's commandments, including His covenant. In the Old Testament, there was a popular Jewish tradition that the tallit and the tassels supported the belief in the coming Messiah.

Jesus, as the coming Messiah, was prophesized as having healing in his wings (Malachi 4:2). If we look at this Scripture in reference to the prayer shawl, Jesus was believed to have the power of healing in the tassels of his prayer shawl, which are attached to the corners (or wings) of the shawl. Some have said that the length of the shawl from corner to corner is the wingspan of an eagle. The Jews believed that when Jesus appeared, the tassels of His prayer shawl were anointed to heal. He publically demonstrated this by ministering healing, as recorded in Luke 8:43-48.

4. **Praying in Agreement**

Praying with others solidifies agreement, which can activate healing, as indicated by this verse:

> Again I say unto you, That if two of you shall agree on earth as touching any thing that they shall ask, it shall be done for them of my Father which is in heaven. For where two or three are gathered together in my name, there am I in the midst of them.
>
> *Matthew 18:19-20*

There is immense power when two or more individuals collectively join their Faith together and engage in prayer (Leviticus 26:8; Deuteronomy 32:30). When you align your Faith with those who are on one accord with your belief for healing, you release the power that causes the spirit of infirmity to flee. The key is coming into agreement with unselfish and committed individuals who genuinely want to sacrifice time through prayer and fasting for your personal healing. It is more than others stating that they will be or they are praying for you. It requires *right now* action because you are needing a *right now* healing.

If any member in your inner-circle of prayer warriors is *not* committed, then there is a breach in your walls of prayer. You need agreement in order to build an *impenetrable fortress* of prayers that cannot be breached for the sake of your healing. The next time you want to affect a change concerning any situation, follow the prayer of agreement rules. It is certainly one of the best ways of praying and getting results.

If you cannot find a prayer group or partner whose consciousness and commitment for healing matches your own, be the source of one with the Holy Spirit. When you and the Holy Spirit become the source, others will be attracted to you, thereby creating the power of agreement in prayer. When two or more are assembled in agreement, it creates a multi-cord that cannot be quickly broken (Ecclesiastes 4:12).

5. Exercising Faith

Healing can be achieved by speaking or praying words of Faith (Mark 11:23). When you speak God's Word, you are releasing Faith into the atmosphere. The Word of God is your mighty weapon against sickness and disease. When His Word of promise becomes fixed in your heart, you will find yourself praying in Faith while giving Him glory for your healing, even when the only signs and evidence you have of His answer are your own words of Faith.

We often pray the words, "Lord I want to be healed." When you pray that way, God could give you the very thing you are praying for: the experience of wanting to be healed. In other words, God will give you the *wanting-ness* of the healing you want. A more effective prayer is a *prayer of gratitude or thanksgiving*. It is not a prayer of pleading, begging, or even wishing. It is your Faith that crosses over into absolute knowing that you are healed. It is your thanksgiving unto the Master Physician who can help to advance your healing.

When you thank the Lord in advance by Faith for what you are expecting, you acknowledge that what you are praying for has already been made manifest. If what you pray for is already real or has been realized supernaturally, your prayer is not a request at all, but it is a statement of gratitude, which makes you whole, as we see in Luke 17:11-19.

If you receive healing through prayer but do not match it with Faith, you are simply repeating what others are saying. Repeating what you hear without Faith only gives you blind-sided hope, not divine healing. Life and death are in the power of your tongue (Proverbs 18:21). Never speak doubt, fear, or death if you truly desire to live in vibrant health. Additionally, do not allow others to speak death over what you have decreed to be health, healing, and life over your life by Faith.

6. **Laying on of Hands**

We can transfer the anointing of healing by the laying on of hands. As a servant of God, you are to faithfully lift up holy hands before God (1 Timothy 2:28). According to the Scripture, we are asked not to just lift up our hands, we are asked to lift up our holy hands. Why? What are *holy hands*? Holy hands are sinless hands that have been dedicated to our Holy God. Holy hands have been set aside for God's use. Holy hands are instruments of blessing for God's glory. So you need to lay *holy hands*, in Jesus' name, on the specific area that is hurting, diseased, or afflicted. Your hands, or any holy hands, are an extension of the hands of Jesus.

The laying on of hands was practiced in the Old Testament. The priests laid their holy hands on the scapegoat to transfer the peoples' sin upon it. Jacob placed his hands upon Joseph's children to bless them. Moses conferred a portion of his wisdom and spirit upon Joshua by laying on his hands.

What do the sick receive when holy hands are laid on them? According to Mark 11:24, they received God's power to be healed. By the laying on of the believer's *holy* hands, healing power is imparted, as demonstrated in the New Testament. Jesus often laid hands on people before healing them (Mark 6:5; Luke 4:40; 13:13). Jesus imparted spiritual and tangible blessings that caused the sick to be healed. The apostles also laid hands upon the sick and they were healed. In fact, the gift of the Holy Spirit can also be administered by the laying on of hands (Acts 4:30, Acts 8:18, 19; Acts 9:17: Acts 19:6).

Therefore, after you pray with holy hands, you can confidently proclaim that you believe that you have received. Your bold confession is not based on what you see or feel. Your confession is based on the solid foundation that it is God's Will for you to be healed. He is a liberal giver of healing power.

> And these signs shall follow them that believe; In my name shall they cast out devils; they shall speak with new tongues; They shall take up serpents; and if they drink any deadly thing, it shall not hurt them; they shall lay hands on the sick, and they shall recover.
>
> *Mark 16: 17:18*

In Acts 28:8, Paul laid hands on a sick person and the person was healed. The act of laying hands on the sick was commonly practiced during the era of the New Testament Church and that same practice is applicable today.

You cannot always be certain that the hands being laid on you are holy. You can, however, cover yourself with a *prayer of protection* just before you are touched by the hands of others. The prayer of protection helps to guard you against anything harmful, thus preventing evil spirits from being transferred onto you.

Here is a sample prayer of protection:

> Father, I thank You for clothing me in Your garment of righteousness and crowning me with a hedge of protection. I decree that no spiritual, emotional, financial, mental, or physical weapon formed against me in any way will prosper. I thank You that I am being protected again evil spirits, curses, or plots devised by principalities, powers, spiritual wickedness, and dark rulers. I thank You that I am rooted, grounded, settled, and established. In the name of Jesus, I pray, AMEN!

7. **Believing**

Mark 11:24 states, "Therefore I say unto you, What things soever ye desire, when ye pray, believe that ye receive them, and ye shall have them." Whatsoever you desire, you need to be sure that it aligns with God's will. When you pray, believe that you have received and provide thanksgiving to the Lord. As soon as you have it by belief, you should not allow your heart to doubt the power of your Faith prayer.

Believing takes unwavering Faith and perpetual patience. Some of your prayers may take a little longer to be answered, but God is Faithful to answer them all. Sometimes, He may not give you what you ask for, but

He will give you what you need, according to His divine and often unarticulated purposes.

When you make up your mind to believe, you set Heaven in motion to back up your belief. With Heaven backing up your belief, you are pushed beyond your natural ability so that you will fully understand, receive, and then walk into your healing.

8. **Using the name of Jesus**

Scripture tells us that saying the name of Jesus rebukes sickness and Satan. Using just the name of Jesus is a powerful healing tool (James 4:7 and John 14:12-13). Jesus gave you power over His Name and the free use of it with the assurance that whatever you ask in His Name shall be given to you (John 14:13-14; 15:16, 26). This demonstrates His trust in you to help manage His Kingdom on the earth. As a born-again believer, you are never acting in the name of someone who is absent. Jesus Himself is not only with the Father on the right hand of the Throne but He is forever present with you. Why? Because He is omnipresent, meaning He is everywhere. His name is mentioned in your sickroom at home, your hospital bed, your doctor's office, your therapy session, the prayer line, and your prayer closet. He is everywhere. When you pray to the Father, it must in Jesus' Name because He is before the Father and so is His name.

With Faith for healing, you can command in the Name of Jesus:
- Deaf ears to be opened
- Cancerous tumors and growths to dry up, die, and disappear
- Tension to cease
- Muscles and nerves to relax
- Migraine headaches to go away
- Pain and affliction to flee
- Swelling to leave
- Demons of affliction to leave
- Arthritis to come out of every joint in the body
- High blood pressure to come down and stay
- Chest pain to go away
- Bones and discs to move into place
- And much more

In the beginning was the Word and the Word was God and Word was with God (John 1:1). The Word was, is, and forevermore will be Jesus Christ. The Word Jesus Christ is the spiritual nourishment you must have to fulfill your purpose. The Bible is called our milk, wine, bread, and meat. It provides a spiritual menu for strength and growth (1 Peter 2:2: NIV). When you step out in

Faith by boldly speaking your authority in Jesus' name, you open the floodgates for healings and creative miracles to come forth.

9. **Meditating on the Word**

Meditating on healing Scriptures is one way of taking God's Word as medicine, which can also result in healing (Proverbs 4:20-22). Meditation on the Word of God involves concentrating and focusing your thoughts on the Word of God (Psalm 119:99). When meditating on the Word, you, as a Christian believer, learn new information, gain greater strength, renew your knowledge, access spiritual truths, and move closer into the presence of God. The words that come out of your mouth will be exactly what God says when you meditate on His Word day and night. When sickness or infirmity makes an entrance into your life, you can strategically escort it out by speaking the Word of God.

When your joy and delight are in the daily meditation upon the Law or the Word of the Lord, you will be like a tree planted by rivers and bring forth much fruit (Psalm 1: 1-3). Daily meditation on His Word can help to bring forth the fruit of healing. When you examine the word *med-i-tate*, you see *med*, as in medicine. God's Word is like medicine. There are a few parallels between God's medicine and natural medicine. God's Word is a healing agent, just as natural medicine is a healing agent or catalyst. In order to be effective, God's Word, like natural medicine, must be taken according to the prescriber's directions. The directions for taking God's medicine are found in Proverbs 4:20, 21 which states, "Attend to them, incline your ear to them, do not let them depart from before your eyes, and keep them in the midst of your heart." Like natural medicine, sometimes you have to give God's medicine time to work.

10. **Obeying the Instructions for the Lord's Supper**

Healing can come by receiving the Lord's Supper in obedience and Faith (1 Corinthians 11:23-30). The Lord's Supper was instituted as a sacrament by Jesus Christ on the night before he went to Calvary. Christ becomes your Passover when you become a worthy participant in the Lord's Supper. When the Israelites ate the lamb, they received healing for their bodies. When you partake in the Lord's Supper, you receive healing for the body, soul, and spirit.

To partake in the Lord's Supper means you engage in a holy communion with the Lord. The word *communion* is derived from the Greek word, Koinonia (Koy-nohn-ee'-ah). Koinonia means to partner, participate, fellowship, benefact, communicate, or intercourse. The act of taking the Lord's Supper, or Communion, represents the act of coming into the intimate presence of the Lord, where the goodness of His benefits are automatically bestowed upon you every day (Psalm 68:19).

Jesus said, "This bread is my body and this wine is my blood which was shed for you" (Luke 11:19; Luke 22:20). The moment you eat the bread and drink the wine, you enter the spiritual presence of Christ. Therefore, you must take caution and go by the Scripture to examine yourself carefully before you take Communion (1 Corinthians 11:28-30). You must ask the Holy Spirit to forgive you of sin and you must be determined not to sin again.

Anything unworthy cannot come before the presence of God's Son because the law of supreme divinity will not allow it (Revelations 21:27). You place yourself in the damnation of further sickness and death if you partake of the Communion unworthily and attempt to go before the Throne (1 Cor. 11:29, 30). Therefore, it is vitally important that you examine yourself before coming into the presence of communing with the Lord. Our loving

God allows space to repent, which enables you to enter His presence, through Communion, with a renewed and clean heart.

5

Receiving and Maintaining Your Healing

*....a time to kill, a time to heal; a time to break down, and a time to build up...**Ecclesiastes 3:1-2***

When you anticipate receiving something, you have to prepare yourself with even greater anticipation to receive it. Preparing yourself can be instant, or it may take some time. Regardless of whether your healing occurs right now or sometime in the future, demonstrating your willingness to receive healing is never in vain. There are four elements or actions for you to consider while you are readying yourself for healing:

1) Positive Relationships;

2) Vision of Healing;

3) Unwavering Faith; and

4) Continuous Thanks.

Let us look at each element of your preparation and your readiness individually.

1. Positive Relationships

Forgive! Forgive others, forgive yourself, and in some cases, forgive God. When you completely empty yourself of un-forgiveness, you remove a vital defense mechanism that is blocking you from obtaining emotional healing and wellness. Your emotional wellness is often the window through which healing will manifest itself in other areas of your life, such as the physical, relational, financial, and spiritual. If you *do not* forgive others from the depths of your heart, then your own sins stand between you and the Father, according to Matthew 6:15.

Yes, you were hurt, abandoned, abused, neglected, ashamed, deceived, tortured, and God only knows what else, but if you allow un-forgiveness to rule your heart, then you will continue to cause hurt, abandonment, abuse, neglect, shame, deceit, and torture to occur within yourself over and over again.

When you do not forgive yourself, you are walking in self-hate, which is one of the most binding emotions you can possess. When an emotion is binding, it confines you, encompasses your being, and even defines you. The fruit of self-hate is fear, depression, anxiety, unworthiness, envy, anger, bitterness, and lack of love. When people have a self-hate nature, they often wonder why no one seems to love or care about them.

Also, you may reflect on why none of your relationships last. People see the fruit of your self-hatred and they distance themselves from you rather than become entangled in your self-directed and negative feelings. If you do not love yourself, or even like yourself, then you give everyone else nothing to like or love about you either. How can someone love you if *you* do not love you?

When you do not forgive God, you send a message that you refuse to trust Him. That is exactly where Satan wants you. Satan wants you to be so distrusting that you will separate your heart from God.

Did you lose a loved one? Did you not get what you wanted from God? Did something not show up as you expected? Whatever it is, you feel as though God has failed you, so you are mad, angry, or upset with the very life force, God Himself, that allows you to breathe right now.

The answer you need is available, but because your heart is so hardened with un-forgiveness against God, you cannot hear what He has to say or see; therefore, and you cannot receive what He has to give to you. I repeat! Forgive others. Forgive yourself. Forgive God. Once you do, you unleash the power needed for healthy and positive relationships to spring forth in your life. Forgiving and creating positive relationships with others, with yourself, and with God make for a merrier heart, which is healing medicine to the spirit (Proverbs 17:22).

If you are in an *unhealthy relationship*, break the soul ties before you are bound in un-forgiveness. Stop trying to resurrect what is dead. Do not redeem a relationship that has expired. If you go beyond the expiration date of a failing relationship, you will only end up with spoiled goods. Anything spoiled is not good for your health.

2. Vision of Healing

Repeat after me, "I am healed!"
"I am healed!"
"I am healed!"

Everything that is spoken after "am" is a creation. Even if you do not believe that at this very moment, get a vision and tell yourself about your vision, first. Tell yourself the vision. What you see or visualize is what you can tell yourself and others. My *vision is waking up without pain*. No one will see your vision unless you tell it. You tell your vision by confessing God's Word daily. You can only confess what is in you, and that is one reason that I wrote this book. I wanted to share healing scriptures, declarations, and prayers. These powerful resources can be in you and in your life, so study them, get them in your spirit, and confess them.

Confession is made with your mouth, and your mouth can have the power to speak life and death (Proverbs 18:21). For example, over and over again, you tell yourself, and others, that your new co-worker, John, does not like you. You are now speaking life into something that your mind will look for even though it does not exist. You have stated something as if it were true. The truth is, though, John, your new co-worker, is shy and intimated by you and almost everyone else at work.

Here is another example:

You developed a nagging pain in your side after you received prayer. You tell people that your pain has not gone away and that you still need prayer and your medicine.

Truth: The sharp pain was your body making an adjustment to line up according to your prayers, but stopped because you aborted the progress when you spoke death, an ending, and not life with regard to your healing. See yourself healed and be sure your words are properly aligned to fit your *visualization*.

3. Unwavering Faith

You must have:
Unwavering Faith
Uncompromising Faith
Bulldog Faith
Hopeful Faith
Faith without evidence
Faith without substance
Long-suffering Faith
Faith
Unwavering Faith

You simply cannot release into the atmosphere what you do not have. Get Faith for your healing. If you need Faith, *read* Faith. Read the Word for your healing. If you need even more Faith, *pray* Faith. Petition God daily for your Faith.

Now Faith is the substance of things hoped for, the evidence of things not seen.

Hebrews 11:1

Who (Abraham) against hope believed in hope, that he might become the father of many nations; according to that which was spoken, so shall thy seed be.

Romans 4:18

He staggered not at the promise of God through unbelief; but was strong in faith, giving glory to God; And being fully persuaded that, what he had promised, he was able also to perform.

Romans 4: 20, 21

But without faith it is impossible to please him: for he that cometh to God must believe that he is, and that he is a rewarder of them that diligently seek him.

Hebrews 11:6

Jesus saith unto him, Go thy way; thy son liveth. And the man believed the word that Jesus had spoken unto him, and he went his way. And as he was now going down, his servants met him, and told him, saying, Thy son liveth. Then enquired he of them the hour when he began to amend. And they said unto him, Yesterday at the seventh hour the fever left him. So the father knew that it was at the same hour, in the which Jesus said unto him, Thy son liveth: and himself believed, and his whole house.

John 4:50-53

Boldly release your Faith by:

- *Commanding* your thoughts and meditating daily on healing scriptures;

- *Articulating* your healing out loud using the Word of God;

- *Committing* to your confession;

- *Resisting* the devil; and

- *Building* your Faith daily.

4. Continuous Thanks

Perhaps one of the most powerful expressions of Faith is to stop praying for healing and simply pray to *thank* God for what you know you have received. By His stripes you are healed (Isaiah 53:5). You *are* healed. *Are* means now! You do not have to worry if you *will be* healed. *Will be* means in the future, but you ARE healed! And His word says you are healed.

The logical response to such a revelation should be, "Thank you, Lord!" Do you realize that God will often heal you in the spirit first before it is manifest in the natural or in your body? Do you also know that your impatience can abort your healing when you start speaking doubts? It is with thanksgiving that we are to let our requests be made (Philippians 4:6).

Your expression of giving thanks can literally shake all of Heaven to move on your behalf. Did you grasp that? Let me say it again, *YOUR* expression of giving thanks can literally *shake all of Heaven to move on your behalf!*

And there is no better story to illustrate this than the story of Jesus healing 20 lepers (Luke

17: 11-19). After Jesus healed them, He told them to go to the priest and show themselves. They had the *vision* of healing and now they had to *tell* someone. They had to *speak* their healing. They had to tell the vision of healing. If you recall that story in the Bible, you know that only one of the lepers came back to tell Jesus, "Thank you."

As a result of that one cleansed leper's heart of thanksgiving, Jesus told him, "I am going to make you whole." Not only was he healed of leprosy, but Jesus spoke one word... whole... and *every* area of the man's life was healed. The man, healed of a horrible, extraordinarily painful, and fatal disease said two words, "Thank you," and the Jesus Christ, the Son of God, said 10 words in reply to him: "Arise, go thy way: thy Faith hath made thee whole" (Luke 11:19). Ten is the establishment of God's law. God was establishing complete wholeness in healing for the humble and grateful man who was no longer a leper.

When you have a forgiving heart, a vision, unwavering Faith, and thanksgiving in your heart, there is no need to ask God over and over again. You simply thank Him. Thank God. Remind Him that you still claim your promise. Praise Him, all the while knowing that He has heard you. Your thankful heart puts God in remembrance of His word, His promise, His Covenant of Healing for you.

6

Ministering Healing to Yourself and Others

*And he said unto them, Ye will surely say unto me this proverb, Physician, heal thyself...**Luke 4:23***

Ministering To Myself: *A Candid Testimony of Healing from the Author*

In 1999, after constantly praying, spending months seeing several doctors, receiving several misdiagnoses, being excessively fatigued, and losing an abnormal amount of weight, I discovered my body was inflicted with non-cancerous stomach tumors. I was attempting to keep my digestive system clean by fasting and using colon cleansers, but I was constantly drinking Mountain Dew as a substitute for water. Mountain Dew soda, which is highly saturated with caffeine and acid, resulted in the destruction of my protective stomach lining and thus a contributing factor to the onset of tumors.

During my medical examination, the doctor quickly prescribed aggressive medicines and warned me to start taking them immediately. I told him that I would need to research the prescribed medicines to fully understand all of the side effects. He told me there was no time! My visibly-frail body was his evidence.

Fear set in as he explained the medicines aggressive purpose, which was to dissolve the tumors, thus leaving noticeable traces of blood in my urine and stool. As he put the written prescription in my hand, his parting words assured me that I would see relief in three wesks.

Three weeks came and went. There was no relief. My fear heightened. The pain grew intense and the blood in my urine and stool was alarmingly excessive. The doctor responded to my new symptoms by telling me I needed to "give it another three weeks." My fear intensified even more.

After three more weeks, the doctor again gave me the same response again. "Three more weeks and you will see relief," he said. By then, I was overcome by fear and hopelessness. My unrecognizable and feeble body, along with the doctor's report, and all my unanswered prayers for healing, collectively persuaded me to accept what I thought was my fate, an untimely and pending death.

I somehow managed to find peace as I recounted the wonderful life God had allowed me to live. The unimaginable accomplishments including international achievements I had earned—ME! A little boy who had grown up in the West End housing development projects of Cincinnati, Ohio. Perhaps I cheated fate too long by becoming something the enemy thought I did not rightfully deserve to be: a successful Christian.

As I recounted all my undeserved blessings, I stopped asking for healing and simply thanked my God for life over and over again. Yes, I continuously wove and intertwined my inner prayer atmosphere with spoken scriptures of *thanksgiving.* I began to look for other people who had health challenges, and despite my own withering health, I prayed for them like I had once stormed Heaven for myself. After praying, I gave after-care instructions to help the recipients of prayer take accountability in the words that I had spoken by the Holy Spirit.

The more I prayed for others and thanked God, the sicker I became, until one night, I lay in bed and I could not move at all. I did not have the energy to call for help. I could not reach the phone that was just inches away on the nightstand. I did not have the strength or stamina to yell or scream for help. I did scream, in the loudest whisper I could manage, but no one could hear. No one was around. My world, my room, my surroundings started to dim slowly.

I realized I could make a slight utterance and I thought, "If I am going to die, I will force my body to praise God." So I kept repeating, "Hallelujah!" Over and over and over. I could not recognize my own murmuring voice, but I just continued praising Him with everything I had. In that precious moment, every tissue, each organ, every membrane, cell, thought, feeling, and every ounce of imagination came alive within me to reverence the Almighty One.

Then, suddenly, it was dark. It was quiet. It was lonely. It was still. And then…there was nothing.

I woke up. At first, I was not sure where I was or how long I had been out. I realized I had not slept, but I had journeyed. Where had I been? Despite my concentrated attempts, I could not remember. What had I experienced? I could not recollect. The more I forced myself to try to remember, the more I began to lose fragments of it. Bits and pieces were becoming abstract and fading away into the distance, like fireflies. Nevertheless, something was different and I was not sure what it was.

I tried to sit up but felt a sharp pain in my side, which quickly reminded me of my health challenge. Just as I was wiping the sleep from my eyes, I heard it. It was an audible voice cautioning me to stop taking all of the medicines. My natural eyes erratically searched the room for the person who spoke to me, but my spiritual enlightenment told me the voice was from within and from above. I had heard the voice of God.

After several days of not taking the medicines, I felt slightly better. In fact, I felt better than I had in months. I finally got the nerve to call my doctor and tell him that God told me to abandon the medicines. My doctor's response was probably the most frightening thing I had encountered yet.

He said, "If you do not continue the medications, you will be in the emergency room in seven days, and in 14 days, we will be burying you there."

The burning fear returned. Perhaps the voice I heard had been imaginary. After all, my doctor was a skilled expert. In that sobering moment, I was standing gingerly on the dividing line of Faith. My choices included Faith in the doctor's report or Faith in my Savior's Word. I begged God for another sign – something I could see, smell, hear, and touch. Anything.

Nothing.

Nevertheless, I decided to stand in Faith, believing in the voice of my Savior. I survived beyond 14 days without the medicines; I lived, despite my doctor's negative prognosis. Although I felt much better, I was still weak and sickly, but I gave God thanks and prayed even more fervently for other sick individuals.

As I was praying for Susan, a woman who was being healed of pancreatic cancer, she told me to go see her doctor, an internal medicine specialist. I did and I brought all my medicines to this new doctor as he had instructed me to do.

He examined the cocktail of medications and quickly concluded that they collectively had brought about an extremely adverse effect in my body. Rather than curing me, the medicine was counter-actively working to burn my insides. Had I continued taking the medicines, it would have resulted in life-threatening or fatal consequences.

How thankful I was to have heard from God and to have obeyed. How thankful I was to have continued to thank him for life while praying heartfelt petitions for others to be healed. The new doctor prescribed one medicine, not several, and I eventually was healed and became whole without surgery.

I was ashamed to initially pray for people, because I, too, was sick. Could a sickly person actually pray for another sick person? Would that make me a hypocrite? Would I transfer the spirit of infirmity, causing greater sickness on those who came to me to get into an agreement for their healings?

No. I had a fight in me. I had deposited far too much Faith in the Word of God concerning my own healing. As individuals were drawing what was in me *out*, it only confirmed my own Faith in my own healing. The more fervently I prayed for others to be healed, a residue of those petitions was added to my own heavenly account. I received a double-fold anointing of healing when I prayed for others.

Ministering Healing To Others

I will never understand it, but it seems easier to pray for others than it is to pray for ourselves. We seem to have more confidence in other external voices praying than our own internal utterances. Admittedly, during my season of sickness, I had often found it easier to enter into the Holy of Holies when praying for my brothers and sisters in Christ. Perhaps it was the pressure of knowing that their forward-looking eyes and steadfast ears were hoping beyond hope in my own Faith to hear from God.

Here are six key points I offer you when you are called to minister healing to others:

1. *Prepare* by Studying and Praying

2. *Identify and Confirm* the Area of Healing

3. *Share* God's Word

4. *Get* Agreement for Healing

5. *Pray* the Word with Authority in Jesus' Name

6. *Implement* an After-Care Plan

1. Prepare by Studying and Praying

Key Scripture References:

Study to shew thyself approved unto God, a workman that needeth not to be ashamed, rightly dividing the word of truth.

2 Timothy 2:15

All scripture is given by inspiration of God, and is profitable for doctrine, for reproof, for correction, for instruction in righteousness: That the man of God may be perfect, thoroughly furnished unto all good works.

2 Timothy 3:16-17

This book of the law shall not depart out of thy mouth; but thou shalt meditate therein day and night, that thou mayest observe to do according to all that is written therein: for then thou shalt make thy way prosperous, and then thou shalt have good success.

Joshua 1:8

Just as you must deposit funds in order to withdraw funds, you have to deposit quality time studying God's Word and seeking His face in order to withdraw His promises. Many people believe when they are praying for healing, that they can simply state what is in their hearts rather than speaking aloud the specific healing Scriptures.

Why is it so important to speak the *logos*, or Word of God? God is a covenant-making God, a covenant-revealing God, and covenant-keeping God. God recognizes and honors His Word, which *is* His Covenant.

Diligently preparing and studying the Word of God allows you to minister with the Holy Spirit and without shame or fear. The Holy Spirit provides guidance and direction for determining the right Words to pray so that healing will be made manifest. Nothing pleases God more than when you carefully speak His written Word. You should regard the written Word of God with the same reverence as the psalmist who wrote, "Thy word is a lamp unto my feet, and a light unto my path." Your efforts to minister in the area of healing are only effective if it flows out of your daily study of the Word and out of your relationship with the Holy Spirit.

2. Identify and Confirm the Area of Healing

Key Scripture Reference:

Ask, and it shall be given you; seek, and ye shall find; knock, and it shall be opened unto you; For every one that asketh receiveth; and he that seeketh findeth; and to him that knocketh it shall be opened.

Matthew 7: 7-8

Bless the LORD, O my soul, and forget not all his benefits: who forgiveth all thine iniquities; who healeth all thy diseases; who redeemeth thy life form destruction; who crowneth thee with loving kindness and tender mercies.

Psalms 103:2-4

As it is written, I have made thee a father of many nations,) before him whom he believed, [even] God, who quickeneth the dead, and calleth those things which be not as though they were.

Romans 4:17

When ministering to others, you may be prompted by the Holy Spirit to troubleshoot the nature of the sickness by asking questions. Usually, when this happens, the Holy Spirit is leading you from the visual, surface manifestation of the sickness to see the spiritual root causes. For example, a woman requesting prayer for breast cancer may need to forgive another woman in her life before healing can be achieved.

Here are some general questions the Holy Spirit may prompt you to ask:

- *How long have you been sick?*

- *Are you on medications for the sickness?*

- *Where is the pain?*

- *Do you believe Jesus can heal you?*

- *Do you have bitterness or un-forgiveness towards yourself, others, or God?*

- *Have you repented and ask God for forgiveness?*

- *Do want to receive prayer for healing?*

- *May I pray for you?*

Remember, Satan does not mind you treating the symptoms with prayer because you are not uprooting the core of the problem. So when the Holy Spirit leads you to stay in a general area, asking specific questions, He is trying to help you identify and confirm the true area of required healing. If you are not sensitive to the direction of the Holy Spirit, Satan will take you off on the *bunny trail* and the results could be fatal for the one needing healing. Notice the two questions that ask the sick individual if he/she wants prayer for healing and if you can pray for them. No matter how strong a prayer warrior you may be, if an individual does not want prayer, a fortress against prayer is established around their hearts.

3. Share God's Word

Key Scripture Reference:

So shall my Word be that goeth forth out of my mouth: it shall not return unto me void, but shall accomplish that which I please, and it shall prosper in the thing whereto I sent it.

Isaiah 55:11

Declare his glory among the heathen, his wonders among all people.

Psalm 96:3

And this gospel of the kingdom shall be preached in all the world for a witness unto all nations; and then shall the end come.

Matthew 24:14

The Word not only creates Faith in the hearts of people, it is the only thing that feeds the spirit, soul, and body.

Hebrew 11:3

When you teach or share the Word of God, you must allow the Word to come forth with the power of the Holy Spirit before placing hands on the sick. When the Holy Spirit is truly present, it removes fear, doubt, and faulty mindsets while preparing the way for physical, emotional, relational, and spiritual healing.

You must be a lover of the Word when you are working the Word. When you work the Word, the

Word will work for you—not *your* words, wishes or pleadings, but the Words from Elohim, the God who created everything by the power of His own Words. Without the Word of God, which is supported by your Faith, you cannot minister effectively. Your prayers will not penetrate beyond the earth realm to reach the Heavenly throne if you do not have the Word and Faith. As you minister to others, do so with authority; work the Word as Jesus did – He sent His Word, and healed them, and delivered them from their destructions (Psalms 107:20).

4. Get Agreement for Healing

Key Scripture References:

Again I say unto you, that if two of you shall agree on earth as touching anything that they shall ask, it shall be done for them of my Father which is in heaven. For where two or three are gathered together in my name, there am I in the midst of them.

Matthew 18:19, 20

Let the word of Christ dwell in you richly in all wisdom; teaching and admonishing one another in psalms and hymns and spiritual songs, singing with grace in your hearts to the Lord.

Colossians 3:16

And five of you shall chase an hundred, and an hundred of you shall put ten thousand to flight: and your enemies shall fall before you by the sword.

Leviticus 26:8

Next to the prayer of salvation, the prayer of agreement is by far one of the most important weapons of spiritual warfare. However, it is vitally important that you choose your prayer partner wisely. Do not hesitate to ask the Lord to lead you to the person or people with whom to come into agreement. The power of the prayer of agreement, which is binding and loosening in His Name, is achieved when two or more prayer partners, with Faith, come into agreement. Without Faith for prayer issues, the power of prayer agreement is non-effective, null, and inoperative.

When you come together with your prayer partner in complete Faith, then Jesus' Word clearly says that it will be done. The more Faith the person you are praying for and the prayer partners collectively have, the greater the outcome of the desired prayer. Faith is maximized when you perform step three of this process, which includes *Sharing the Word* to create at least two witnesses in the earth realm (Matthew 18:19). If nothing else, this Scripture suggests there is little to no power when we stand alone as *lone rangers* in the Kingdom of God.

5. Pray the Word with Authority in Jesus' Name

Key Scripture Reference:

I will worship toward thy holy temple, and praise thy name for thy loving kindness and for thy truth: for thou hast magnified thy word above all thy name.

Psalm 138:2

If ye shall ask any thing in my name, I will do [it].

John 14:14

If ye abide in me, and my words abide in you, ye shall ask what ye will, and it shall be done unto you.

John 15:7

The Word of God is magnified above His name. Although the grass withers, the flower fades, the Word stands forever.

Isaiah 40:8

God is doing more than protecting the reputation of His Word; He is a Father protecting his Son. According to John 1:1, "In the beginning, was the Word (Jesus) and the Word was with God, and the Word was God.

When you pray in the name of Jesus, you are releasing the highest level of authority in all of creation, both in the visible and in the invisible realms, to uphold your prayer requests for healing. God, the Father, gave Jesus the Christ all authority over thrones, principalities, powers, dominions, and might and every named sickness, including the sickness you are conquering by your Faith and prayers.

6. Implement an After-Care Plan

Key Scripture Reference:

Wherefore, my beloved, as ye have always obeyed, not as in my presence only, but now much more in my absence, work out your own salvation with fear and trembling.

Philippians 2:12

Blessed is the man that heareth me, watching daily at my gates, waiting at the posts of my doors.

Proverbs 8:3

Even so Faith, if it hath not works, is dead, being alone.

James 2:17

Joyce, a 48-year-old woman, had corrective surgery to remove ruptured fallopian tubes, which were causing her excruciating pain. The three-hour procedure was a success, but Joyce was required by her doctor to stay at the hospital for two days. On the day of her release from the hospital, the doctor gave her a prescription for two types of medications. He also required her to come to his office once a month for the next four months. Joyce left the hospital feeling relieved that the surgery went well and confident in the doctor's follow-up plan.

Having a medical procedure like surgery is only part of most individuals' journey to healing. Some type of after-care regimen is needed to ensure that the healing process is working or to identify complications as early possible. Early detection will maximize opportunities to correct any problems.

In short, when you pray for others, you are inviting the Holy Spirit to conduct spiritual surgery. Imagine that once the prayer, the spiritual surgery, is over, you send that person on his or her way without an after-care plan. You might think, no big deal. Well, think again. What if the doctor had sent Joyce home immediately after the surgery on her fallopian tubes? Like most people, you would question the actions of the doctor and medical staff to release Joyce far too early because she was still vulnerable after surgery.

Do you know the same logic applies to anyone who gets prayer? The minute you release someone after you have prayed without any after-care treatment, no Word, no directions, and no *spiritual* antibiotics, you leave the person open for Satan to steal, kill, and destroy. Here are a few ideas to consider prescribing to anyone you pray over:

- *Continue* to share the word of God.

- *Recommend* one or more full gospel churches.

- *Provide* Bible Scriptures for the individual to meditate on daily.

- *Donate* a Bible to the individual.

- *Suggest* an accountability partner or partners.

- *Invite* the individual to your church.

- *Offer* your contact information for future communications (or recommend another prayer partner) to confirm the healing is occurring or modify the aftercare healing plan

7

Healing Prayers for You

For I will restore health unto thee, and I will heal thee of thy wounds, saith the Lord
Jeremiah 30:17

Prayer is the Living Word of God spoken from our lips. His Word is alive, operative, energetic, effective, and it is sharper than any two-edged sword. Every time you articulate God's Word, you release everlasting life and Faith into the atmosphere. In fact, all of Heaven recognizes the Word of God when it is spoken from our mouth. When you hold His Word up to Him in prayer, the Lord will not only hear His Covenant Word but He will see Himself and His Son (John 1:1-5).

These powerful healing prayers are designed to encourage, to strengthen, and to heal you and any loved ones to whom you provide care. Pray continuously with Faith. Then you will get to know Jehovah Rophi more intimately as the Lord who heals you (Exodus 15:26) and strengthens you in every situation Here are eight healing prayers for your use:

1. Prayer for Salvation
2. Prayer for Healing and Health
3. Prayer for Defeating Bad Habits
4. Prayer for Overcoming Emotional Hurts
5. Prayer for Honoring Leaders
6. Prayer and declaration for Binding, Loosening, and Breaking
7. Prayer for Declaring God's Lordship
8. Prayer of Adoration and Thanksgiving

1. Prayer of Salvation

Heavenly Father, in the Name of your son Jesus Christ, I repent of every sin in my life and ask that You will forgive me for being disobedient to Your Will and Your Word. I confess my sins right now. You are Faithful and just in every situation. I believe You will forgive me and cleanse me from all unrighteousness. I confess with my mouth that Jesus is Lord over my life. I believe in my heart that You raised Him from the dead. I ask Your Son, Jesus Christ, to come into my heart now.

I welcome the Holy Spirit into my life. I believe I am reborn and I am saved now and forevermore. I now have redemption through the blood of Jesus Christ. All my sins, iniquities, and transgressions have been forgiven according to the riches of His grace. In the Name of Jesus, I pray. AMEN!

2. Prayer for Healing and Health

Father, in the Name of Jesus, I come boldly before the throne of grace to confess Your Word concerning my health and healing. Your Word states that You will forgive all of my iniquities and heal all of my diseases. You desire, above all things, that I would prosper and be in good health. Therefore, I ask that You forgive me for allowing fear, un-forgiveness, self-rejection, guilt, rebellion, self-hatred, sin, pride, and bitterness to open the door to any sickness or infirmity in my life. I repent and renounce all these things, in the name of Jesus.

I stand confidently on Your Word over my entire body because Your Son was wounded for my transgressions, He died for my sins, He was buried for my iniquities, and the chastisement of my peace was upon Him. With His stripes, I am healed from the top of my head to the soles of my feet. I decree that every cell, every organ, every tissue, and every system in my body is lining up to operate according to Your original purpose. The mountain of infirmity against my body has been uprooted and no longer has residency in my body. I cast out every lingering and hidden spirit of sickness and disease that may be lurking secretly in my body.

I render all evil spirits in my body to be ineffective, inoperative, powerless, and dead. I decree and declare that I am completely and totally healed from the crown of my head to the soles of my feet. My entire body lines up with Your Will and operates in the manner in which You created it.

Lord, as I continue to pray and confess Your Word concerning my healing, my light shall break forth in the morning and my health shall spring forth speedily as Your righteousness goes before me. Now Father, as I have spoken Your Word over my life for healing, I receive Your Healing Covenant for my life. I hold fast to my confession of Your Word and I stand immovable, knowing that health and healing are mines, NOW! In Jesus' Name, I pray. AMEN!

3. Prayer for Defeating Bad Habits

Father, by Your authority, I decree and declare that I am a new creature. Old things are passed away and all things have become new. The old me was nailed to the Cross with Your Son, Jesus Christ, in order that my body might be made dead unto all bad and sinful habits. I was buried with Him in Baptism and I was raised together with Him by the power of the Holy Spirit so that I might live each day and behave in the newness of life.

Your Son redeems and protects my life from every attack. He crowns me with loving kindness and tender mercies. In Him, I live and have my being. I have been delivered from the control and dominion of darkness; I have been transferred into the Kingdom of Light. I have been crucified with Christ. Nevertheless, I live, yet not I, but Christ lives in me.

I am an overcomer. I overcome all evil, temptations, addictions, and strongholds through the power of Jesus Christ. Because Greater is Jesus Christ who lives, abides, and dwells in me, than the enemy who is in the world. Death no longer has power over Jesus and sin has no dominion over me. Bad habits are now under His feet. He is far above principalities, powers, and rulers of the darkness of this world and wicked spirits in high places. I have complete victory. AMEN!

4. Prayer for Overcoming Emotional Hurts

Heavenly Father, You sent Jesus to heal the brokenhearted. You sent Him to set the captives free. I plead in the name of Jesus that You will grant me complete emotional healing from both the past and current hurts.

Despite my challenges, I receive Your unspeakable joy and everlasting peace, which passes all understanding. Every care, every weight, and every attack I lay down right now and follow you. In You, I have the strength and the understanding to resist the spirits of anxiety, abuse, anger, envy, depression, bitterness, hopelessness, loneliness, fear, and guilt.

Where the spirit of the Lord is, there is liberty. I am liberated in You. I thank You for mending my broken heart from every hurt today. I no longer have an emotional weight and I walk in the newest of Your marvelous light. And right now, I accept Your unwavering peace, which transcends all emotional wounds and guards my heart and mind. In the Name of Christ Jesus, I pray. AMEN!

5. Prayer for Binding, Loosening, and Declaring

I have the Keys of the Kingdom, and whatever I bind on Earth is bound in heaven. Whatever I loose on Earth is loosed in heaven.

I bind, rebuke, and renounce every known and unknown open door for religious spirits and their works of darkness in my life.

I bind, rebuke, and renounce all slandering against the moving of the Holy Spirit in my life.

I bind, rebuke, and renounce every spirit of deception and error in my life.

I bind, rebuke, and renounce every stronghold and demonic influence in my life.

I bind, rebuke, and renounce the spirit of deception and hypocrisy in my life.

I bind, rebuke, and renounce all pride, arrogance, and self-righteousness in my life.

I loose the spirit of obedience and truth over, in, and on my life.

I loose the ministering spirits of God over my life.

I loose the spirit of health in my body, mind, and soul.

I loose the powers of Peace, Truth, Love, and Joy into my life.

I loose Wisdom, Knowledge, and Revelations into my life.

I loose Peace over my home, finances, relationships, and possessions.

I loose greater Faith over my life.

I loose the Seven Spirits of God into my life.

I break up the fallow ground in my life and decree the glory of God forevermore.

I break every ungodly soul tie.

I break every ungodly generational tie in my family line.

I break every curse and vow.

I break the weight of guilt and shame.

I break every hex.

I break every spell.

I break the stronghold of un-forgiveness and rejection.

I break every incantation, worldly ritual, and ungodly tradition.

I break every ungodly covenant, agreement, and allegiance.

I decree that I am free!

I declare that I am free!

I decree and I declare that I am Free forevermore!

In the Name of Jesus. AMEN!

6. Prayer for Honoring Leaders

Father, I pray for all those who have authority: the President, Vice President, elected and appointed officials, spiritual leaders, heads of every household, educators of the youth, and supervisors. I pray for leaders so that I will lead a more quiet and peaceable life in all godliness and all honesty according to your Word. I pray that all leaders and all the people will humble themselves, pray, seek Your face, and turn from their wicked ways so that they will hear from heaven, receive forgiveness for their sins, and witness the healing of the land. May our leaders flow continuously in the Holy Spirit. I pray that the anointing of God is evident in all that they do. May they walk in Divine health all the days of their lives.

I pray that Angels are surrounding them like a mighty shield. May there be a spiritual hedge of protection around the health, finances, marriages, families, and ministries of our leaders. I declare that wisdom, favor, prosperity, and the peace of God are abounding in their lives. Father, give them the desire to study, understand, and follow the principles of Your Word. May they realize that all authority comes from You, not from men, and that one day they will stand before You to give an account of their actions while in the earth realm.

I pray that you will rebuke Satan, the father of lies, for his deception that mankind can make decisions without consulting You. I pray that leaders will trust in you with all of their hearts and that they will lean not on their own understanding. I pray that they will acknowledge You in every thought and deed. May You continue to direct their paths.

I pray for our Constitution, our military, and political leaders. Bless teachers who teach our children and parents who rear them. Give all leaders wisdom and courage. Father, may You continue to be glorified on the earth and in the church by Jesus Christ forevermore. In the name of the One who holds the entire world in His hands, by the power and authority of the Lord Jesus Christ, I pray. AMEN!

7. Prayer for Declaring God's Lordship

Father God, I invite You now to be: Lord over my spirit, soul, and body; Lord over my thoughts, imaginations, words, and actions; Lord of my emotions and reactions; Lord over my physical body, which is your temple; Lord over my eye gates, nose gate, ear gates, and mouth gate; Lord over my hands and all that I touch; Lord over my feet and everywhere step; Lord over my sexuality and identity;

Lord over my home, my family, and my relationships; Lord over my finances, my tithes, my offerings, and my possession; Lord over my time, my sleep, my work, and my service for You in the Kingdom of God; Lord over my desires, needs and wants.

You and You alone are my Lord and Master. I declare your mighty Word over my life as I receive Your restoration, love, and strength. I now stand strong in You and the power of Your might. In the Name of Jesus, I thank you. AMEN!

8. Prayer of Adoration and Thanksgiving

Heavenly Father, I thank You because this is the day that You have made. I will rejoice and be glad in it. I run to Your gates with thanksgiving and I dance in Your courts with praise. I serve You with gladness and recognize that You are The Supreme Lord of everything. From the rising of the sun to the going down of the same, You are the Alpha and the Omega; the first and the last; the author and the finisher of all things. Your ruling scepter of righteousness rules over all principalities, powers, dominions, and might.

Every knee shall bow down and every tongue shall confess Your Lordship. All things consist by You and You consist in all things. Without You, nothing that was made was made. You are the Great I AM who reveals Himself daily. There is nothing that You cannot do and will not do for those who love You for Your namesake. All of Your promises are yes in Christ Jesus because you are a covenant-making, covenant-revealing, and covenant-keeping Lord. Your Word shall never fade or wither away; rather it will perform everything You send it out to accomplish.

Your Kingdom is an everlasting Kingdom. Your dominion will endure forever. Men shall speak of Your glory and power for generations to come. You are greater than powerful. As King David said, Your loving kindness is better than life. I pause right now from everything to honor You, to adore You, and to energize myself in You.

Great is your Faithfulness, my Lord. Your greatness is unsearchable and never-ending. In Your mighty hand is the power to make great and to give strength to all. The greatness of Your steadfast love never ceases. I choose to praise You all the days of my life because of Your worthiness. Your tender mercies are new each and every morning. Your mercy and goodness follow me this day and all the days of my life. Your Eternal Kingdom is the power and the glory forever. In the mighty name of Jesus, I pray. AMEN!

8

Declaring Life: *100 Healing Scriptures*

*I shall not die, but live, and declare the works of the LORD...**Psalm 118:17***

God says in His Word, "Faith comes by hearing and hearing by the Word of God." Therefore, in order to build Faith to receive healing, you must hear the Word on the subject of healing so that the Faith for healing will come. This is the purpose of Scriptures.

Be sure you look up the verses of Scripture for yourself. Meditate on them daily. Put *your* name in the Scriptures and make them specific to your personal need. Jesus said in Matthew 9:29, "According to your Faith be it unto you." If your Faith is there for healing, healing will be made manifest.

Your Scripture usage should be greater than your vocabulary. Release the prayer of Faith in the Scriptures you speak. You can start each week by meditating on three new healing Scriptures for yourself. Confession is good for the soul, so repeat your weekly healing Scriptures over and over. But do not just hang on the Scriptures in silence; speak them out in the atmosphere to release the Word of healing from your inner core.

You speak the Word of God to keep your healing. Say the whole. Complete Word of God because Faith *is* the complete WORD of God. We normally say, "By His stripes, I am healed," but there is more to it. Daily meditation on healing and healing Scriptures is required.

As you get closer to your Heavenly Father through His Son Jesus, you shall "know" the truth that sets you free. If you stay in fear, you are not made perfect in Love. It is Love that casts out all fear, which results in God's Love (I John 4:18). If you are not living in Faith and speaking the Truth, then fear, not love, will manifest all sorts of physical, mental, and spiritual problems in your life (Proverbs 26:2).

Here are 100 healing Scriptures to help you strengthen your Faith for healing. Be sure to choose a few each week to meditate upon and to also speak into the atmosphere:

1. **Isaiah 41:10** - Fear thou not; for I [am] with thee: be not dismayed; for I [am] thy God: I will strengthen thee; yea, I will help thee; yea, I will uphold thee with the right hand of my righteousness.

2. **Job 5:26** - Thou shalt come to [thy] grave in a full age, like as a shock of corn cometh in his season.

3. **2 Chronicles 7:14** - If my people, which are called by my name, shall humble themselves, and pray, and seek my face, and turn from their wicked ways; then will I hear from heaven, and will forgive their sin, and will heal their land.

4. **2 Kings 20:8-9** - And Hezekiah said unto Isaiah, What [shall be] the sign that the LORD will heal me, and that I shall go up into the house of the LORD the third day?   And Isaiah said, This sign shalt thou have to the Lord, that the Lord will do the thing that he hath spoken; shall the shadow go forward ten degrees, or go back ten degrees?

5. **1 Samuel 12:16** - Now therefore stand and see this great thing, which the LORD will do before your eyes.

6. **Deuteronomy 32:36** - For the LORD shall judge his people, and repent himself for his servants, when he seeth that [their] power is gone, and [there is] none shut up, or left.

7. **Jeremiah 17:14** - Heal me, O LORD, and I shall be healed; save me, and I shall be saved: for thou [art] my praise.

8. **1 Peter 2:24** - Who his own self bare our sins in his own body on the tree, that we, being dead to sins, should live unto righteousness: by whose stripes ye were healed.

9. **Isaiah 53:5** - But he [was] wounded for our transgressions, [he was] bruised for our iniquities: the chastisement of our peace [was] upon him; and with his stripes we are healed.

10. **Jeremiah 33:6** - Behold, I will bring it health and cure, and I will cure them, and will reveal unto them the abundance of peace and truth.

11. **Psalms 103:2-4** - Bless the LORD, O my soul, and forget not all his benefits: who forgiveth all thin iniquities; who healeth all thy diseases; who redeemeth thy life from destruction; who crowneth thee with lovingkindness and tender mercies.

12. **James 5:14** - Is any sick among you? let him call for the elders of the church; and let them pray over him, anointing him with oil in the name of the Lord:

13. **James 5:15** - And the prayer of Faith shall save the sick, and the Lord shall raise him up; and if he have committed sins, they shall be forgiven him.

14. **Matthew 10:1** - And when he had called unto [him] his twelve disciples, he gave them power [against] unclean spirits, to cast them out, and to heal all manner of sickness and all manner of disease.

15. **James 5:16** - Confess [your] faults one to another, and pray one for another, that ye may be healed. The effectual fervent prayer of a righteous man availeth much.

16. **3 John 1:2** - Beloved, I wish above all things that thou mayest prosper and be in health, even as thy soul prospereth.

17. **Philippians 4:19** - But my God shall supply all your need according to his riches in glory by Christ Jesus.

18. **Matthew 10:8** - Heal the sick, cleanse the lepers, raise the dead, cast out devils: freely ye have received, freely give.

19. **Proverbs 17:22** - A merry heart doeth good [like] a medicine: but a broken spirit drieth the bones.

20. **Psalms 127:3** - Lo, children [are] an heritage of the LORD: [and] the fruit of the womb [is his] reward.

21. **Deuteronomy 7:15** - And the LORD will take away from thee all sickness, and will put none of the evil diseases of Egypt, which thou knows, upon thee; but will lay them upon all [them] that hate thee.

22. **Romans 5:3-4** - And not only [so], but we glory in tribulations also: knowing that tribulation worketh patience; And patience, experience; and experience, hope:

23. **Hebrews 11:6** - But without Faith [it is] impossible to please [him]: for he that cometh to God must believe that he is, and [that] he is a rewarder of them that diligently seek him.

24. **Isaiah 54:17** - No weapon that is formed against thee shall prosper; and every tongue [that] shall rise against thee in judgment thou shalt condemn. This [is] the heritage of the servants of the LORD, and their righteousness [is] of me, saith the LORD.

25. **Proverbs 16:24** - Pleasant words [are as] an honeycomb, sweet to the soul, and health to the bones.

26. **Matthew 11:28** - Come unto me, all [ye] that labour and are heavy laden, and I will give you rest.

27. **Proverbs 4:20-22** - My son, attend to my words; incline thine ear unto my sayings. Let them not depart from thine eyes; keep them in the midst of thine heart. For they are life unto those that find them, and health to all their flesh.

28. **James 4:7** - Submit yourselves therefore to God. Resist the devil, and he will flee from you.

29. **Isaiah 57:18** - I have seen his ways, and will heal him: I will lead him also, and restore comforts unto him and to his mourners.

30. **Hebrews 11:1** - Now Faith is the substance of things hoped for, the evidence of things not seen.

31. **2 Corinthians 12:9** - And he said unto me, My grace is sufficient for thee: for my strength is made perfect in weakness. Most gladly therefore will I rather glory in my infirmities, that the power of Christ may rest upon me.

32. **John 10:10** - The thief cometh not, but for to steal, and to kill, and to destroy: I am come that they might have life, and that they might have [it] more abundantly.

33. **Luke 4:18** - The Spirit of the Lord [is] upon me, because he hath anointed me to preach the gospel to the poor; he hath sent me to heal the brokenhearted, to preach deliverance to the captives, and recovering of sight to the blind, to set at liberty them that are bruised.

34. **Matthew 7:7-8** Ask, and it shall be given you; seek, and ye shall find; knock, and it shall be opened unto you; for every one that asketh receiveth; and he that seeketh findeth; and to him that knocketh it shall be opened.

35. **Psalms 34:20** - He keepeth all his bones: not one of them is broken.

36. **Psalms 6:2** - Have mercy upon me, O LORD; for I [am] weak: O LORD, heal me; for my bones are vexed.

37. **Deuteronomy 32:39** - See now that I, [even] I, [am] he, and [there is] no god with me: I kill, and I make alive; I wound, and I heal: neither [is there any] that can deliver out of my hand.

38. **Hebrews 13:8** - Jesus Christ the same yesterday, and today, and forever.

39. **Numbers 6:25-27** - The LORD make his face shine upon thee, and be gracious unto thee: The Lord lift up his countenance upon thee, and give thee peace. And they shall put my name upon the children of Israel, and I will bless them.

40. **1 Corinthians 11:1-34** - Be ye followers of me, even as I also [am] of Christ.

41. **Luke 10:9** - And heal the sick that are therein, and say unto them, the kingdom of God is come nigh unto you.

42. **Matthew 13:58** - And he did not many mighty works there because of their unbelief.

43. **Matthew 28:18-20** – And Jesus came and spake unto them, saying, all power is given unto me in heaven and in earth. Go ye therefore, and teach all nations, baptizing them in the name of the Father, and of the Son, and of the Holy Ghost: Teaching them to observe all things whatsoever I have commanded you; and, lo, I am with you always, even unto the end of the world. Amen.

44. **Matthew 9:27** - And when Jesus departed thence, two blind men followed him, crying, and saying, [Thou] Son of David, have mercy on us.

45. **Matthew 4:23** - And Jesus went about all Galilee, teaching in their synagogues, and preaching the gospel of the kingdom, and healing all manner of sickness and all manner of disease among the people.

46. **Jeremiah 30:17** - For I will restore health unto thee, and I will heal thee of thy wounds, saith the LORD; because they called thee an Outcast, [saying], This [is] Zion, whom no man seeketh after.

47. **Isaiah 57:18-19** - I have seen his ways, and will heal him: I will lead him also, and restore comforts unto him and to his mourners. I create the fruit of the lips; Peace, peace to him that is far off, and to him that is near, said the Lord; and I will heal him.

48. **Psalms 51:1- 3** - Have mercy upon me, O God, according to thy loving kindness: according unto the multitude of thy tender mercies blot out my transgressions. Wash me thoroughly from mine iniquity, and cleanse me from my sin. For I acknowledge my transgressions, and my sin is ever before me.

49. **Psalms 41:4** - I said, LORD, be merciful unto me: heal my soul; for I have sinned against thee.

50. **Numbers 12:13** - And Moses cried unto the LORD, saying, Heal her now, O God, I beseech thee.

51. **James 5:11** - Behold, we count them happy which endure. Ye have heard of the patience of Job, and have seen the end of the Lord; that the Lord is very pitiful, and of tender mercy.

52. **Acts 28:27** - For the heart of this people is waxed gross, and their ears are dull of hearing, and their eyes have they closed; lest they should see with [their] eyes, and hear with [their] ears, and understand with [their] heart, and should be converted, and I should heal them.

53. **Acts 4:30** - By stretching forth thine hand to heal; and that signs and wonders may be done by the name of thy holy child Jesus.

54. **Acts 4:21-22** - So when they had further threatened them, they let them go, finding nothing how they might punish them, because of the people: for all [men] glorified God for that which was done. For the man was above forty years old, on whom this miracle of healing was shewed.

55. **Luke 5:17** - And it came to pass on a certain day, as he was teaching, that there were Pharisees and doctors of the law sitting by, which were come out of every town of Galilee, and Judaea, and Jerusalem: and the power of the Lord was [present] to heal them.

56. **Matthew 17:20** - And Jesus said unto them, Because of your unbelief: for verily I say unto you, If ye have Faith as a grain of mustard seed, ye shall say unto this mountain, Remove hence to yonder place; and it shall remove; and nothing shall be impossible unto you.

57. **Matthew 13:15** - For this people's heart is waxed gross, and [their] ears are dull of hearing, and their eyes they have closed; lest at any time they should see with [their] eyes, and hear with [their] ears, and should understand with [their] heart, and should be converted, and I should heal them.

58. **Ecclesiastes 3:1-3** - To every [thing there is] a season, and a time to every purpose under the heaven: A time to be born, and a time to die, a time to plant, and a time to pluck up that which is planted; A time to kill, and a time to heal; a time to break down, and a time to build up.

59. **Job 5:17-18** - Behold, happy [is] the man whom God correcteth: therefore despise not thou the chastening of the Almighty: For he maketh sore, and bindeth up: he woundeth, and his hands make whole.

60. **1 Peter 2:21-24** - For even hereunto were ye called: because Christ also suffered for us, leaving us an example, that ye should follow his steps: Who did no sin, neither was guile found in his mouth; Who, when he was reviled not again; when he suffered, he threatened not; but committed himself to him that judgeth righteously; who his own self bare our sins in his own body on the tree, that we, being dead to sins, should live unto righteousness; by whose stripe ye were healed.

61. **Ephesians 4:1-32** - I therefore, the prisoner of the Lord, beseech you that ye walk worthy of the vocation wherewith ye are called.

62. **2 Corinthians 7:1** - Having therefore these promises, dearly beloved, let us cleanse ourselves from all filthiness of the flesh and spirit, perfecting holiness in the fear of God.

63. **2 Corinthians 5:7** - For we walk by Faith, not by sight.

64. **2 Corinthians 1:3** - Blessed [be] God, even the Father of our Lord Jesus Christ, the Father of mercies, and the God of all comfort.

65. **1 Corinthians 12:9** - To another Faith by the same Spirit; to another the gifts of healing by the same Spirit.

66. **Isaiah 57:19** - I create the fruit of the lips; Peace, peace to [him that is] far off, and to [him that is] near, saith the LORD; and I will heal him.

67. **Isaiah 19:22** - And the LORD shall smite Egypt: he shall smite and heal [it]: and they shall return [even] to the LORD, and he shall be intreated of them, and shall heal them.

68. **Ecclesiastes 3:11** - He hath made every [thing] beautiful in his time: also he hath set the world in their heart, so that no man can find out the work that God maketh from the beginning to the end.

69. **Psalms 119:77** - Let thy tender mercies come unto me, that I may live: for thy law [is] my delight.

70. **Psalms 119:71** - [It is] good for me that I have been afflicted; that I might learn thy statutes.

71. **Psalms 119:50** - This [is] my comfort in my affliction: for thy word hath quickened me.

72. **Psalms 119:40** - Behold, I have longed after thy precepts: quicken me in thy righteousness.

73. **Psalms 119:28** - My soul melteth for heaviness: strengthen thou me according unto thy word.

74. **Psalms 119:25** - DALETH. My soul cleaveth unto the dust: quicken thou me according to thy word.

75. **Psalms 107:41** - Yet setteth the the poor on high from affliction, and maketh [him] families like a flock.

76. **Psalms 103:1-5** - Bless the LORD, O my soul: and all that is within me, [bless] his holy name. Bless the Lord, O my soul, and forget not all his benefit: Who forgiveth all thine iniquities; who healeth all they diseases; who redeemeth thy life from destruction; who crowneth thee with lovingkindness and tender mercies; who satisfieth they mouth with good things; so that thy youth is renewed like the eagles.

77. **Psalms 41:1-3** - Blessed [is] he that considereth the poor: the LORD will deliver him in time of trouble. The Lord will preserve him, and keep him alive, and he shall be blessed upon the earth; and thou wilt not deliver him unto the will of his enemies.

78. **Psalms 41:3** - The LORD will strengthen him upon the bed of languishing: thou wilt make all his bed in his sickness.

79. **Psalms 35:27** - Let them shout for joy, and be glad, that favour my righteous cause: yea, let them say continually, let the LORD be magnified, which hath pleasure in the prosperity of his servant.

80. **Psalms 34:6** - This poor man cried, and the LORD heard [him], and saved him out of all his troubles.

81. **Ephesians 2:2** - Wherein in time past ye walked according to the course of this world, according to the prince of the power of the air, the spirit that now worketh in the children of disobedience:

82. **Galatians 3:14** - That the blessing of Abraham might come on the Gentiles through Jesus Christ; that we might receive the promise of the Spirit through Faith.

83. **1 Corinthians 11:1-5** - Be ye followers of me, even as I also [am] of Christ. Now I praise you, brethren, that ye remember me in all things, and keep the ordinances, as I delivered them to you. But I would have you know, that the head of every man is Christ; and the head of the woman in the man; and the head of Christ is God. Every man praying of prophesying, having his head covered, dishonoureth his head.

84. **Romans 4:17** - (As it is written, I have made thee a father of many nations,) before him whom he believed, [even] God, who quickeneth the dead, and calleth those things which be not as though they were.

85. **Acts 4:16** - Saying, What shall we do to these men? For that indeed a notable miracle hath been done by them [is] manifest to all them that dwell in Jerusalem; and we cannot deny [it].

86. **Acts 4:10** - Be it known unto you all, and to all the people of Israel, that by the name of Jesus Christ of Nazareth, whom ye crucified, whom God raised from the dead, [even] by him doth this man stand here before you whole.

87. **Acts 2:41-43** - Then they that gladly received his word were baptized: and the same day there were added [unto them] about three thousand souls. And they continued steadfastly in the apostles' doctrine and fellowship, and in breaking of bread, and in prayers. And fear camp upon every soul: and many wonders and signs were done by the apostles.

88. **Luke 14:4** - And they held their peace. And he took [him], and healed him, and let him go;

89. **Luke 13:13** - And he laid [his] hands on her: and immediately she was made straight, and glorified God.

90. **Luke 13:12** - And when Jesus saw her, he called [her to him], and said unto her, Woman, thou art loosed from thine infirmity.

91. **Luke 10:19-20** - Behold, I give unto you power to tread on serpents and scorpions, and over all the power of the enemy: and nothing shall by any means hurt you.

92. **Luke 8:48** - And he said unto her, Daughter, be of good comfort: thy Faith hath made thee whole; go in peace.

93. **John 4:47** - When he heard that Jesus was come out of Judaea into Galilee, he went unto him, and besought him that he would come down, and heal his son: for he was at the point of death.

94. **Romans 12:2** - And be not conformed to this world: but be ye transformed by the renewing of your mind, that ye may prove what [is] that good, and acceptable, and perfect, will of God.

95. **Romans 12:1-2** - I beseech you therefore, brethren, by the mercies of God, that ye present your bodies a living sacrifice, holy, acceptable unto God, [which is] your reasonable service. And be not conformed to this world: but be ye transformed by the renewing of your mind, that ye may prove what is the good, and acceptable, and perfect, will of God.

96. **Acts 10:38** - How God anointed Jesus of Nazareth with the Holy Ghost and with power: who went about doing good, and healing all that were oppressed of the devil; for God was with him.

97. **John 14:27** - Peace I leave with you, my peace I give unto you: not as the world giveth, give I unto you. Let not your heart be troubled, neither let it be afraid.

98. **John 12:40** - He hath blinded their eyes, and hardened their heart; that they should not see with [their] eyes, nor understand with [their] heart, and be converted, and I should heal them.

99. **Luke 7:7** - Wherefore neither thought I myself worthy to come unto thee: but say in a word, and my servant shall be healed.

100. **Mark 1:30-31** - But Simon's wife's mother lay sick of a fever, and anon they tell him of her. And he came and took her by the hand, and lifted her up; and immediately the fever left her, and she ministered unto them.

The End

.....but *your beginning* of a new outlook on obtaining physical, emotional, and spiritual wholeness.

A Note to You...

Dear Reader,

I have prepared this closing message just for you. Never lose your hope in hope and keep Matthew 19:26 close to your heart. Continue pressing beyond doubts, fears, and traditional church teachings. *Breaking the Healing Code* can potentially lead to your final breakthrough. It is never too late to be who you were meant to be – completely healed and abundantly happy.

Visit my website for additional information, to complete a reader's survey, submit a speaker request, get occasional free download offers, or sign up for future products, upcoming books in the Breaking the Code series, event announcements, and so much more.

Finally, thank you for reading my book! If you enjoyed it, please consider leaving a positive book review on Amazon.com or Goodreads.com. Remember, I am standing in agreement with you for your healing, prosperity, and growth in the Lord!

From your friend and author,

Christopher-Charles Chaney
www.AuthorChristopher.com
AuthorChristopher@yahoo.com

PS
Join our "Breaking the Code" family by emailing me your selfie with a full view of your purchased book, a quote, and permission to use your submission to promote the book's mission of physical, emotional, and spiritual wholeness within the Kingdom of God.

Meet Your Author...

Christopher-Charles Chaney strategically developed one of the most successful federal sustainable acquisition programs in the USA when he was a senior program manager and marketplace minister for the Federal Government. Chaney is the CEO and pastor of the Kingdom Majesty International Ministries, which is headquartered in Chattanooga, TN. He is also an award-winning speaking champion, international award winning designer, a national advocate for caregivers and the author of the Mama Peaches and Me book reading series.

He is also a certified Purpose Development Coach and Consultant specializing in helping Christians find their unique purposes in the Kingdom of God. Chaney has an MBA from the University of Cincinnati. His diverse gifts have made it possible for him to minister not only in the USA, but also Paris, France; Copenhagen, Denmark; Gifu, Japan; and Jamaica. His heartfelt passion is to lead people in discovering their purpose on earth and in the Kingdom of God.

To request Christopher-Charles Chaney as a speaker, submit a book review, read his other books, join the mailing list, complete a reader's survey, and more, please visit www.AuthorChristopher.com.

Breaking the Healing Code by Christopher-Charles Chaney named the Number One Hot New Release in Christian Bible Study Guides!

Amazon.com
Spring 2015

www.ingramcontent.com/pod-product-compliance
Lightning Source LLC
LaVergne TN
LVHW051236080426
835513LV00016B/1613